THINGS THEY DON'T
WANT YOU TO KNOW

Also by Ben Brooks

The Impossible Boy

Stories for Boys Who Dare to be Different 2

Stories for Kids Who Dare to be Different

Stories for Boys Who Dare to be Different

Everyone Gets Eaten

Lolito

Grow Up

The Kasahara School of Nihilism

An Island of Fifty

Fences

THINGS THEY DON'T WANT YOU TO KNOW

Eleven Lessons for Raising
a 21st-Century Teenager

Ben Brooks

Quercus

First published in Great Britain in 2020 by

Quercus Editions Ltd
Carmelite House
50 Victoria Embankment
London EC4Y 0DZ

An Hachette UK company

A CIP catalogue record for this book is available
from the British Library

HB ISBN 978 1 52940 394 7
TPB ISBN 978 1 52940 393 0
Ebook ISBN 978 1 52940 392 3

Based on an idea by Blackie Books.

Contents

Introduction

If you're reading this, you probably have children, and these children may be in the process of growing taller, sulkier, and hairier around the genitals. This blossoming also happened to me. I know it happened to you too, I'm not stupid, * but mine occurred fairly recently† and so probably bore more of a resemblance to what your angelic offspring are currently going through.

While in some respects teenagers today are just as hopeful, hopeless, and hard-headed as any of the generations that have come before them, in other ways they are the first of their kind. They are guinea pigs; the first people not to know life without super-fast internet, ever-present smartphones and relationships shaped by social media. They are the first not to understand what it ever meant to live unconnected by the omnipresent web of the

---

* Yesterday I found out Atlantis wasn't real.

† A kind and gentle man first suggested I write a version of this book when I was twenty-two. By the time you're reading this, I shall be at least twenty-eight.

digital realm, and we are only just starting to see just how deeply its effects are being felt.

The world has changed, and the experience of coming of age within it is changing too. We used to talk about children growing up too fast, though we barely acknowledge this any more. It has become a given. How long can you stay a child when all it takes to research 'anal creampie' is a few flicks of the thumb? How do you keep young people safe when even their most raucous friends' disgusting jokes pale in comparison to the extreme ideas lurking behind computer screens? How do you keep any of the world's horrors at bay from a kid with access to the internet?

The last decade has transformed adolescence, and that is why I'm writing this book.

I want to help you understand what it's like to be a teenager in an age of self-harm, selfies, and sexting. I want to help you help your kids. I want to do this because I know how hard it was and how much easier it could have been.

As my transition from prepubescent caterpillar to pizza-faced butterfly unfolded, I watched my parents panic and flounder with questions they were unprepared for. Is the computer killing his brain? Is *Grand Theft Auto* making him want to pistol-whip prostitutes? Does he have friends? Is he watching porn? What does he do on that phone? What are those cuts up his arms? Why are his pupils so big? What are we supposed to do?

My parents inherited child-rearing tactics from their own parents and quickly realized that these had become useless. Anything physical would mean a call to Childline, followed by high-pitched threats of legal action. Grounding doesn't mean much if your friends live in your phone. Taking the phone away doesn't mean all that much either when you've got a laptop upstairs. And you're not taking the computer, Mum, because otherwise I won't be able to do any homework, will I? And is that what you want? For me to end up getting three GCSEs, doing media studies in Plymouth, moving back home and living with you until you die?

Anyway, how do you punish someone who's already so miserable?

You've probably read that levels of anxiety, depression, and self-harm amongst young people are at an all-time high. Figures from the Office for National Statistics show that suicides amongst girls aged sixteen to twenty-four increased by 83 per cent in the six years leading up to 2019, and NHS figures show a 48 per cent rise in anxiety and depression in British children over the past fifteen. Yet you'd be hard pressed to argue that these kids aren't the most tolerant, socially aware, and generally well-informed group of pubescents ever to grumble about being woken up at seven every morning. Young people are drinking less,* smoking less,† and having less risky sex than the generations that came before them.‡ They are generally less afraid of being open about sexuality and mental health than their forebears. They're even punching each other less than they used to.§

---

* In 2018, the Epidemiology and Public Health department of University College London found that, between 2005 and 2015, the number of non-drinkers aged sixteen to twenty-four rose from 18 per cent to 29 per cent.
† 2019 NHS Digital data showed 16 per cent of 13,000 eleven-to-fifteen-year-olds had smoked a cigarette in their lifetime, down from 49 per cent in 1996.
‡ The Office for National Statistics figures show teenage pregnancy was halved in the sixteen years leading up to 2016.
§ According to a study by UCL and the University of Liverpool, the number of fourteen-year-olds who punched or kicked someone on purpose fell from 40 per cent to 28 per cent over the past ten years.

So what's happening?

I'm not entirely sure. I am not a scientist or a sociologist or even a person that wakes up before noon, but I did survive being a teenager at a time when porn replaced the birds and the bees, new drugs were invented faster than they could be banned, and over a third of kids announced that their future dream job would involve telling a webcam what they'd eaten for breakfast.*

The internet taught me how to shave and dance and have sex. Most nights I fell asleep cradling a phone. At sixteen, I started taking fluoxetine, switched to citalopram, tried olanzapine, and settled on beer. My first girlfriend lived in the computer. My drug dealer lived in the computer. My sense of self-worth was almost entirely dependent on the computer.

It's possible I wasn't an average teenager, if there is such a thing, which means my experiences might serve more as a warning than anything else. Then again, it's also possible that your offspring are just better at hiding things than I ever was.

You may be shaking your head at this point. 'But I know my son/daughter', you might think, 'and they are kind and clear-headed and they don't keep anything from me'. Well, I'm glad. Sceptical, but glad. The number of times I have heard 'my Oscar would never do that' is directly proportional to the number of times I have witnessed, first-hand, your Oscar doing exactly that. Not in any sinister way, just because a part of growing up has always meant establishing an identity separate from your parents,

---

* A 2017 survey by travel company First Choice found that 34 per cent of kids wanted to be YouTubers when they grow up.

and this generally involves a certain amount of lying: 'I won't leave our postcode, there's nothing in my pocket, and I'm staying at Archie's tonight.' (Still, there are parents who insist their children are unfailingly honest with them. Apparently it doesn't take long to forget how it felt to be a teenager.)

The problem with ignoring the fact that kids are going to gravitate towards certain things – drugs, sex, stealing Mars bars from supermarkets – is that they are going to get guidance about it from somewhere, and if it isn't from you, it might prove dangerous. For example, if you have a son, you're probably not going to tell him not to try and fit his entire fist into a girl during his first sexual encounter, but porn* is going to positively encourage him to do that. Later, when he attempts this desperately sexy manoeuvre on an unsuspecting young woman, she'll likely hit him and/or end up developing a small vagina complex as a result of having seen the very same porn.

What's the solution? You probably haven't (until now) imagined your son considering fisting, let alone thought about how best to break it to him that it isn't how we do things in the real world. Confronted with the unexpected, parents, teachers, uncles, and aunts panic, and often respond in ways that make things worse.

When my parents discovered a diary in which I was chronicling self-harm, my deepest secrets were hand-delivered to a flustered

---

* You may not think your child has seen porn. In which case you are probably wrong. A 2019 BBFC study found that three quarters of parents think their kids hadn't seen porn, while 66 per cent of fourteen-to-fifteen-year olds said they had. The other 34 per cent were probably lying, by the way, because they thought it might get back to their parents.

geography teacher (see chapter 9). While I was downing activated charcoal in a post-overdose hospital bed, I was lambasted with furious accusations of selfishness and idiocy. Drinking – on the other hand a true marker of adolescence – went almost entirely unpunished, because here was something that was knowable, familiar, and therefore made sense, while being caught with a carrier bag of nitrous oxide canisters was an offence punishable by two weeks' banishment from home.

I don't blame my parents. Apart from drinking to giggly oblivion, these teenage pastimes were not things that they had any experience of. Their confusion led to anger, frustration, mis-communication, and a certain amount of unnecessary pain. It was a shame. It hurt. It put me beyond the reach of help when I needed it most. Once trust in your parents evaporates, it can be a difficult thing to restore, and it's a dangerous thing for a teenager to try and cope without that lifeline.

When my contemporaries' kids reach their acne years, hopefully there won't be such a gulf. They will have had their own experiences with sending nudes, being dumped on Messenger, and talking about mental illness without acting like it's a recent invention of attention-seeking children. They will be able to offer advice. They will, perhaps, understand* because although every generation feels a world away from the one before it, you'd struggle to deny that the arrival of the internet hasn't done a great deal to widen that gap.

Until then, the aim of this book is to tell you something about

---

* It's also possible that everything will continue to change exponentially, and the next generation will wrestle with biotech, matrix-style brain uploads, and the ethics of boning aliens.

how I grew up, something about how everyone else is growing up, and try to offer up a few suggestions for how best to ease the friction of it all. If this generation of kids is having trouble, they'll need a hand from the adults around them, which is unfortunate because young people aren't always thrilled about asking for help. The best I can do is tell you what would have worked for me, my friends, and the kids I interviewed for this book. (Rory, Kelly, Simon, Samson, and Erica are some of the fake names I invented for some of the kids that I spoke to while trying to get a fuller picture of teenage life today. They ranged in age from thirteen to seventeen and came from different parts of the UK, as well as slightly further afield.)

Alongside their mumbled testimonies, I checked statistics, read books, and tried to decode incredibly dull studies in an attempt to see whether any of it applied to reality. Sometimes it did. Sometimes it didn't. But the eleven lessons that follow are my best attempt at setting out how it feels to grow up today and what it might be helpful for you to understand if you're going to help the ones you love reach adulthood relatively unscathed.

So this book is for confused parents. It's for anyone who is custodian of a teenager currently feeling lost, alone, depressed, horny, in need of another body, or like they want to relocate to another planet. And it's also, indirectly, for the young me, and for Katie Connor, * who, after that video leaked, had to move to a school three counties away.

---

* Not her real name. There will be no real names in this book, except for mine and those of various rappers.

Will it help?

It might do, somehow. But it will not be a parenting guide written by someone who was already stockpiling Werther's Originals when computers first started infiltrating our homes. It will be a look at modern life through the eyes of a teenager, by someone who recently graduated from that club and is more than happy to take you on a tour of the sites that most parenting manuals would rather pretend don't exist. There is porn, there are hallucinogens, and kids do call each other cumstains on the internet. None of those things signal the end of the world, but to remain completely unaware of their existence can mean you end up getting blindsided if they ever do crop up. And blindsided people rarely make wise choices.

Anyway, you have nothing to lose, except for the money spent buying this book and the time it takes you to read it. If it doesn't help, there will at least be a few pages about the medicinal properties of various herbal teas and a handful of reading suggestions to make sure there are some useful takeaways between this introduction and the acknowledgements.

I am not a teenager any more. I survived my adolescence, just like you did, and just like your kids will. But it is possible to hit twenty with a minimum of scarring, no criminal record, and a functioning relationship with your parents. At least that's what I've heard.

Lesson One:

Don't Let Your Kid Become a Commodity

Phones, computers, and the real world

I

Oscar: You there?

Adam: Yeah, why?

Oscar: Just bored.

Adam: K.

Oscar: What did you have for dinner?

Adam: Lasagne. You?

Oscar: Haven't had it yet.

Adam: Did you do the maths sheet?

Oscar: Not yet. Did you?

Adam: No. I might just say I got lasagne on it.

'No phones at the dinner table, please,' says Oscar's mum.

'What?'

Oscar becomes furious at the interruption. He's thinking: Why do I have to put my phone away at the dinner table? I'm messaging my actual human friends, something you might understand if you actually had any, but you don't, because you are literally the worst person who has ever existed.

'Put it away please, poppet,' his mum says. 'Just while we eat.'

Adam: You there?

Oscar: Sorry, I have to go, my mum is being a massive stupid bitch.

II

Every morning, I wake up and immediately check email, Gmail, Twitter, Facebook, the *Guardian*, the *Daily Mail** and podcast updates. The same is true of almost everybody. Eighty per cent of smartphone users check their phones within fifteen minutes of opening their eyes. I'd be surprised if the figure wasn't higher for teenagers. Every single under eighteen I talked to while writing this book said they slept with their phone under their pillow or within arm's reach, and instantly began scrolling come morning. For some, wanting to spend longer in bed on their phone often came at the expense of showering or eating breakfast.

---

*   If you know the enemy and know yourself, you will not fear the result of a hundred battles. – Sun Tzu

Why? Teenagers are generally not waiting for important emails, generally don't have work that needs doing at 7 a.m. and are generally not hugely invested in the stock markets or news from the other side of the world. For the most part, these kids are messaging friends they'll see in approximately forty minutes' time while going through notifications that have accumulated during the night. Their phone is telling them, here is what you missed while you were wasting your time sleeping, idiot: Saira hit the gym, Declan is planning to go to Crete, Dan snapchatted you a picture of his two-foot-long turd, and Kanye West has been cancelled for asking why slaves didn't just sucker-punch their owners and go build castles in the Appalachian mountains.

The truth is, teenagers have a fear of missing out that can trump almost anything else. It is why they will climb out of a bedroom window at night, get in a car with a drunk driver, swim in a freezing pond, or scale a church while high on psychoactive drugs. It is also why they are the perfect target for social media platforms. If they don't constantly check their phone they might miss out on something, and that would be the end of the world.

At the very start of the day, Oscar has already heard about all the terrible things that have happened in the world overnight, seen which of his friends is having a better time than him, clocked that he doesn't have as many likes on a new picture as he had on the last one, missed breakfast, and been subjected to the close-up image of a loose acquaintance's freshly popped whitehead.*

---

* Spot popping is very popular on the internet. YouTube videos of particularly large examples being burst have garnered over twenty million views each.

He listens to hyper-aggressive hip-hop through his phone as he gambols towards the ugly building where his mind is to be moulded. Every now and again, the songs are interrupted by the plinks and blips of snapchats and Facebook notifications.

At school, he periodically slides his phone out and taps at it under the desk. Eventually, a teacher will notice. Once again the same conversation that, at any given moment, is being played out in thousands of schools, unfolds as if scripted and learned by heart.

Teacher: What are you doing under the desk, Oscar?

Oscar: Nothing, sir.

Teacher: I hope that's not a phone.

Oscar: What do you hope it is, sir?

Teacher: Don't be cheeky. Raise your hands.

(Oscar cautiously raises his hands.)

Teacher: Now stand up.

Oscar: Do I have to, sir?

Teacher: Just stand up.

(He stands up, phone falling off his lap and onto the ground.)

Teacher: And what's that on the floor?

Oscar: It's a calculator, sir.

Teacher: Is it, really?

Oscar: Yes, sir, I swear.

Teacher: Well, you can collect your calculator from the office after school.

Oscar feels fidgety and restless for the rest of the lesson. He keeps thinking he feels a vibration in his pocket but when he thrusts his hand in there he finds it's empty. He wonders if someone's trying to get in touch with him. What if Elia wants to go to the cinema? What if there's been an unprecedented windfall of likes on that joke he made about wanting to stab himself in the leg with a compass?

At break time, everyone else is on their phones and he stares morosely into the palms of his hands. He usually has a phone to keep him occupied. What is he supposed to do or think about now? He spends double chemistry doodling engorged dicks in the margins of a dog-eared exercise book.

On being reunited with his phone, he finds that there are no new messages or notifications. But how can that be possible? He hasn't touched it in four hours. Nothing's happened since then? No one cares that he exists? They care about everyone else, he can see that, they've liked everyone else's photos.

In goes Trippie Redd singing 'Mac 10', and so begins the sulk home. Once he gets back, he collapses onto his bed and flicks through social media for a few hours. Bikinis, talent shows, new songs, old songs, trailers, tractors, needy dogs, basketball dunks.

Why is Keegan allowed to go on holiday during term time? Don't parents get arrested for that? And why is Simon taking pictures in the gym? He still looks like a weed. Pip hasn't replied but she's read his message. Why wouldn't she reply? She knows he knows she's seen it. And she'll know he knows she knows he knows. Is she playing a game?

Eventually Oscar's mum's head appears in the doorway.

'Poppet,' she says. 'Are you doing your homework?'

'I'll do it now.'

'No, darling, you'll do it now.'

'That's what I said.'

'We both know that we don't mean the same thing when we say "now".'

Sighing dramatically, he flips open a maths textbook to page 44, exercise 8a. Which angles are supplementary angles? What the fuck is a supplementary angle? Supplementing what? And what's that drawing supposed to be?

He asks Google what supplementary angles are. As he's doing that, he gets a message.

Adam: What are you doing on Saturday?

Oscar: Idk, I have to go to my stupid nephew's stupid baptism.

Adam: Baptisms are the worst.

Oscar: My mum is being a massive bitch about it.

Adam: Say you're ill.

Oscar: She never believes me that I'm ill.

Adam: I wish we had periods. Then we could just not go to stuff and blame it on our periods.

Oscar: That would be sick.

Adam: Have you seen this?

(Oscar clicks on a link to a video of an enraged McDonald's customer hurling her Big Mac at a server's face from point-blank range.)

Oscar: Yeah, I saw it already.

(Which doesn't, by the way, stop him from re-watching it again in its entirety.)

Oscar turns back to his exercise book, one that he's stolen from the maths cupboard at school. He's written the date and the page number and the word 'Homework'. He puts in earphones and plays Death Grips. He starts a documentary on his tablet and idly watches a grey-haired man in tweed amble along the Jurassic coast.

His mum's head reappears. Her mouth is moving.

He pulls out an earphone.

'What?' he shouts.

She looks hurt.

'I said how can you concentrate with earphones in, while watching the TV and being on your phone?'

'It's called multitasking.'

'I wouldn't be able to do anything with all that going on.'

'Well, I can.'

(Actually, he can't. Studies have shown that multitasking is a myth. You cannot concentrate on the TV, your maths homework, and the music in your ears, any more than you could concentrate on the instruction manual for a printing press from 1898. The human brain isn't capable of it.)

After dinner, Oscar watches a few hours of predictable crime drama on Netflix. At eleven, he's told to go to bed.

He turns off the lights.

He struggles to sleep. He always struggles to sleep. He lies awake scrolling through Twitter on his phone. When it turns 2 a.m., he plays an ASMR* video of a woman scrunching up plastic bags to help him drift off. It works, but he wakes up at 4 a.m. when a message bleeps in.

Adam: Apparently Connor Tipton has a foot fetish.
Oscar: Really?

At seven thirty he wakes up and checks his phone again. He feels like shit. He refuses to get out of bed until the last minute, when he necks a coffee in the kitchen and promises himself a nap during triple physics.

I've lived this day a thousand times over, as has everyone born after 1990.

III

Though the particulars might change, for better or for worse, our days and nights are being shaped by computers.

YouTube has become the introduction to the internet that most kids now receive. When the grown-ups want to have some peace

---

* ASMR stands for autonomous sensory meridian response. It generally involves videos or sound recordings of people speaking in whispers, eating soft foods, or gently caressing things. ASMR can be calming, arousing, or both. A 2015 study by Barratt and Davis found that 98 per cent of people who used ASMR did it 'for relaxation.' It might be something to try next time you're out of ways to look busy at work.

and quiet, young Oscar and his sister Emma are given the iPad and told to occupy themselves by trawling through the bottomless online repository of videos ranging from decades-old cartoons to the gaffes committed by politicians a few minutes earlier.

The square-eyed siblings know the machine well. It's been a staple of their lives since birth, propped up in front of their hypnotized faces to keep them from moaning that they're bored.

They'll watch cartoons, they'll watch videos of kids watching other videos, videos of adults eating spicy foods, videos of other adults trying and failing to bake impressive cakes. They'll watch kids their own age opening Christmas presents. They'll watch deranged re-imaginings of *Peppa Pig*, saturated with blood and guts. They'll watch rap parodies of songs they've never heard the originals of. They'll watch fifteen-minute vlogs* about someone's hair or house or what they ate that day.

My ten- and twelve-year-old nephews watch videos of new football boots being delicately lifted out of their boxes. My eleven-year-old brother will watch fifteen-minute-long videos of planes taking off or landing. Make-up tutorials are hugely popular, particularly amongst kids who don't wear make-up. Video game playthroughs are also massive, especially for those too young to purchase the games in question.

In short, kids fucking love YouTube. According to a 2018 Ofcom report, half of UK children now prefer watching it to television. Instead of having to sit through hours of cartoons they don't like to get to the ones they do, they can gleefully skip from

---

* Video blogs, granddad.

favourite clip to favourite clip. All they need to do is hit a key and move on to the next video. It caters perfectly to their limited attention spans.

By the time they're teenagers, their heroes and role models have been replaced by other young people merrily waving into webcams to them and ten million other kids. These YouTubers are almost entirely unknown by parents, but wield an incredible amount of influence over the lives of children and teenagers, simply because they can make giant lasagnes out of one hundred Big Macs, goad punches out of strangers and taser dead rats. Every couple of months, a YouTuber is included in the cast of pseudo-celebrities sent to eat donkey dicks in the jungle or crack their pelvises while pirouetting on ice.

'Who's that?' anyone over twenty asks.

'A YouTuber,' anyone under eighteen replies, rolling their eyes.

One of the problems with these YouTubers as role models for young children is that they are bulletproof. When PewDiePie says 'Death to all Jews' or Logan Paul wanders around a famous suicide spot in Japan looking for dead bodies, there is no one to pull them up on it. Sure, pockets of the internet might be briefly outraged, or they might be given temporary bans, but this has no long-lasting impact on them or their fan bases. Parents can't be expected to vet every sparkly-toothed American their child is spending time with online, and children in turn aren't going to switch allegiances in light of controversies they barely understand. YouTubers persist in posting their videos, kids carry on watching them, and large amounts of cash continue to be generated off the back of adverts. Where adults are being fired from multinational corporations and universities for misjudged jokes or years-old tweets, YouTubers answer to no one. As long as kids keep watching, they keep making money. A lot of it. The highest earning YouTubers make upwards of $10 million a year.* A game in which you try to turn your character into a famous vlogger – *Youtubers Life OMG!* – has been downloaded over a million times and is now available on Xbox and PS4.

I can only imagine that the lives of these online superstars will not live up to their expectations, even if the pay cheques do. Rates of stress, depression, and burnout will inevitably be huge, considering the constant pressure to produce new content and to increase the numbers of subscribers and followers in such an impossibly competitive field. They spend entire days alone in their homes, trying to look euphoric on camera for an army of thirteen-year-olds around the world, the line between their lives and their online personas blurring into nothing. Kids alone in their rooms waving at other kids alone in their rooms.

IV

While YouTube is becoming the television of the twenty-first century, Snapchat may well be on its way to assuming the mantle of primary mode of communication between the young. Created by a team of university students in 2011, the initial point of the

---

* According to a 2019 *Forbes* list of the highest-paid YouTubers, eight-year-old Ryan Kaji had the highest-earning channel, with its star making over twenty-six million dollars between 1 June 2018 and 1 June 2019.

app was to let people send photos that would disappear a few moments after being seen by the recipient. Presumably the hope was that:

- The impermanence of the pictures would mean that you would not get hung up on achieving perfection.
- It didn't matter if something wasn't particularly funny or interesting, or even if it was offensive or misjudged, it would soon be gone.
- You could send dicks, butts, vaginas, and boobs without having to worry that they would become masturbation fodder for the wrong people.

It's most often used for the sending of customized photos or short videos, overlaid with a few words and glittery cartoon graphics, which sounds cute but isn't necessarily so. A girl, let's call her Candice, might take a brief video of her friend, let's call her Stacey, announcing that she's starving. Candice might then raise the pitch of Stacey's voice, tack a couple of dog ears onto her head, and write 'Stacey smells like dog shit' over the top of it, before sending it to over one hundred of her closest friends. It might be funny, it might not. It might be forgotten, but equally, it might not.

Also, it became clear that nothing was really transient. Many people realized that any received picture could be screenshotted and saved on the recipient's phone. Snapchat 'fixed' this in 2012 by adding a feature that let the sender know if their picture was screenshotted at the other end. However, there are a huge number of workarounds. You can download third-party apps that will happily take screenshots or record videos without letting the sender know. You can disconnect from the Wi-Fi, screenshot, clear app data and reconnect. You can also just take a photo of your phone with another phone. Snapchat might offer the illusion of impermanence but, like so much else that's online, it isn't.

One of the more troublesome aspects of the app is Snapmaps, which shows your exact location unless you specifically turn it off. Another is Snapstreaks, which is a tool designed solely to keep kids messaging each other for as many consecutive days as possible. At the time of writing, Snapstreaks have been a feature of the app for 1,699 days. The longest verified Snapstreak is 1,501 days.* Your reward for crossing the 1,000-day mark? A 1,000-day fire emoji, suitable recompense for three years of non-stop communication.

I was recently having dinner at my nan's when she asked my cousin why exactly she was taking a photo of an empty coffee mug.

'It just needs to be a picture of something,' replied my cousin. 'I'm not breaking my Snapstreak.'

And Snapstreaks are just one of the huge arsenal of psychological techniques used by social media companies, apps and sites like YouTube to keep users logged on for as long as possible. They compete with each other for the time and attention of your children, so that the finite minutes and hours of their lives can be sold as advertising space to companies hawking shoes, make-up,

---

* I've had to update this since starting work on this book. According to techzillo. com, the 1,501 record is held by 'Patrick and Ryan'.

and headphones. They race to create the most addictive possible experiences in order to generate more and more money for Silicon Valley billionaires to spend on cryogenics and edible clay*. Entire departments exist within these companies solely to develop new ways of keeping your children hooked. And they've been busy.

Some of their wonderful creations include:

- **Likes** or their equivalents, which hijack our dopamine systems and prey on the desire of young people to be accepted and validated. You'll spend time thinking of things that will get likes, you'll spend time waiting for likes to appear, and you'll expend energy worrying about not getting likes. The best-case scenario? You get an unusual number of likes then devote even more time and energy to chasing the short-lived dopamine high that accompanied it.
- The **three dots** that let you know someone is typing mean you're obviously going to wait around to find out what inane thing they have to say.
- **Seen** features mean you know someone else has seen your message, and they know you know this, and so they feel pressure to reply as quickly as possible, forcing conversations to continue indefinitely.
- **Infinite scroll**, meaning you never have to click 'next page' and never have a reason to cease mindlessly absorbing useless content. The inventor of infinite scroll, Aza Raskin,

---

* There is, in fact, some debate as to whether the clay is edible. But this does nothing to stop celebrities eating it in the hopes that it will mystically detoxify their heavily-insured bodies.

has since said he feels guilty for his creation, though he explained it away by saying 'in order to get the next round of funding, in order to get your stock price up, the amount of time that people spend on your app has to go up.'

- **Autoplay** on YouTube means the next suggested video will automatically start playing, as it will with Netflix, unless you actively go into the settings and switch the function off. With Facebook, things are even worse. Any advertising video purporting to be something else will automatically start playing once you scroll to it. Because these adverts, tutorials, and trailers are so well targeted, it's more likely than ever that you will, at the very least, passively sit through them. I tend to get shown visually exciting science experiments and videos of bearlike men dead-lifting hundreds of kilograms. These are two entice-ments that I am powerless to resist.

- **Push** notifications which call out from our phones at inopportune moments and let you know you've received messages or notifications, without letting you know what those messages or notifications are, so that of course you're going to log in to the apps in question to find out what's waiting for you.

With all of these techniques, it's no wonder that the average teenager spends over seven hours per day staring at a screen.*

---

* According to a 2019 Common Sense Media poll of US teens, seven hours was the average amount of time spent staring at a screen.

That is how the system works. Your children are being manipulated and exploited for profit. It's no wonder that I pick up my
phone first thing in the morning. And it's no wonder that, during
a talk at Stanford University's Graduate School of Business, the
former vice president of user growth for Facebook said that his
children 'aren't allowed to use that shit' and that he feels 'tremen-
dous guilt' for having created something that is 'ripping apart the
social fabric of how society works'.

V

Where once children might have run away from home to show
their anguish, these days they're increasingly likely to lock themselves in their own bedrooms with their laptops. In this way, social
media has at least played a part in distracting kids from drinking
in public and trading strains of herpes behind bike sheds.

But at what point do we start worrying that it has gone too
far? At what point does this benign blue-lit babysitter become an
obsession that needs controlling?

The phenomenon of *hikikomori* was first noticed in Japan in
the 1990s when large numbers of young people began refusing
to come out of their bedrooms. These teenagers and twenty-somethings were opting out of a society where pressures to
conform and work ceaselessly were unparalleled. They cloistered
themselves in the homes of their parents and simply refused to
participate.

It was not a passing trend. By the 2000s, up to a million

young Japanese people were thought to be *hikikomori*. It led to the Japanese Ministry of Health, Labour, and Welfare coming up with a proper definition for *hikikomori*, which was when a person:

1. Stays at home almost entirely.
2. Does not engage in social activities like going to school or working.
3. Has been in this state for at least six months.
4. Has no clear psychiatric illness or a significantly lower than average IQ.
5. Has no close friends.

Current estimates suggest 1–2 per cent of people under thirty in Asian countries are *hikikomori*. Although not mentioned in the above guidelines, I'm hazarding a guess that for some of these people, their situation is the result of an internet addiction that has spiralled out of control. Surely it is no surprise that the boom in reclusiveness has coincided with the appearance of affordable home computers and immersive games consoles.

You can just imagine how it happens: they might at first spend a few hours a day on the computer, then start getting sucked into it for longer and longer periods, until eventually they give up everything apart from the computer. It's easy to fall through the rabbit hole, especially if you don't have a job to go to or you're not part of an offline friendship group. You get trapped in a cycle. Most *hikikomori* tend to sleep all day and stay up all night, at least in part because of the havoc that unending screen time wreaks on circadian rhythms.

I can see the spiral. I know how easy it is to fall through the rabbit hole, especially when the real world might feel like a cold and uninviting place. During bouts of depression from the age of fourteen onwards, I used to resort to spending several days doing nothing but lying in bed and staring at a screen. Sometimes this involved playing MMORPGs*, sometimes it was watching YouTube videos or reading articles about serial killers, near-death experiences, and the hierarchy of angels. Actually, the important thing wasn't what I was doing, it was that my brain could avoid its own thoughts. In the same way that alcohol can blot out reality for a while, I could also scroll, listen, watch, and read my way into oblivion.

When you feel depressed or alienated, you often cease to value your own time and you become more than happy to waste it on things that you know will prove unfulfilling. The kings of pixellated magical kingdoms, the ill-informed but highly opinionated, the creators of videos in which kettlebells are dropped from helicopters and onto antiques: when low, I was willing to give my time away to anyone who asked. I convinced myself that this was a break from life, a kind of rest to recharge the batteries. Really, it was just gorging on brightly packaged junk food. There is no break from anything, just lazy surrender, a waste of the finite hours we're given. This is life too, the time spent doing nothing on a computer; it's just life that doesn't feel like life.

---

* Massively multiplayer online role-playing game. The kind where you run around dressed in a tabard, collecting gold coins, and getting incinerated by dragons. The most popular amongst them, *World of Warcraft*, has over seven million players.

The *hikikomori* phenomenon is no longer confined to Japan.*
Numerous cases are chronicled all over the world. Although it
was once thought to be inextricable from the unique culture of
Japan, this position now seems difficult to justify.

In one essay, the novelist Ryu (not Haruki) Murakami writes:

> Yet this malfunctioning of communication has nothing to
> do with Japan's 'uniqueness,' some essence inherent in its
> history or tradition that sets it apart from other nations. The
> cause of the malfunctioning is more simple. It is the fact that,
> by the 1970s, we had already achieved the national goal. We
> had worked hard to restore the country from the ruins of
> World War II, develop the economy and build a modern
> technological state. When that great goal was attained, we
> lost much of the motivating force that had knit the nation so
> tightly together. Affluent Japanese do not know what kind of
> lifestyle to take up now. That uncertainty has pulled people
> further apart and caused a whole raft of social problems.
> Hikikomori is naturally one of them.

It's a theory that has been put forward in a number of countries to account for various situations, the gist of it being: maybe
young people today are drifting because they have no fucking
idea what to do.

It feels like the old milestones that provided a clear structure to

---

* Kato (2012) conducted a survey of 124 mental health professionals in eight
countries, all of whom could report cases that matched the description of *hikikomori*.

life are disappearing: people aren't getting married, buying houses, or having children the way they used to. They are less likely to commit to one job or even one sector of work for a protracted period of time. There are more and more articles about how kids are told they can do anything and be anyone they want to be when they grow up. Now many of them are standing idly around clutching expensive university degrees that only a fraction of them will ever even pay off. The confidence they've been pumped full of throughout school is leaking away. Soon enough, they realize they cannot all have the lifestyle they'd imagined they'd have. That sense of entitlement to success combined with a lack of focus, and the realization that the world is far less convinced of their unique abilities than their parents were, is bewildering.

If young people feel like the world doesn't have a place for them, it makes sense that they will stop looking for ways to fit into it. They have more than enough excuses and ways to keep themselves occupied. As distant companies with bottomless reserves of money compete to make ever-more addictive online experiences, it wouldn't be much of a surprise if the growing numbers of young people choosing to log in and drop out multiply in ways we would never have suspected.

Even if we feel a million miles from a *hikikomori* epidemic, kids are spending more time staring at screens, which generally means more time spent indoors. A 2018 study carried out by Persil,* claimed that by the time a British child is seven, they'll

---

* I assume the point was to scare parents into shooing their kids into the muddy outdoors, thus trebling the weekly detergent bill.

have spent double the amount of time looking at a screen (456 days, on average), than they will have spent playing outside. This isn't just unhealthy, it marks the formation of a habit that will be all the more difficult to shake off for having begun so early, at a time when kids are helpless to resist. Some people grow up having never learned to stop sucking their thumbs, chewing their nails, or picking their nose; I, like many other people of my age, have grown up without ever learning how to disconnect from the online world.

VI

Despite everything, in the OECD survey 'Children and Young People's Mental Health in the Digital Age', 84 per cent of students said that they found social media very useful. And it is. It can undoubtedly connect, delight, educate, and inspire. Expats let their families know they're safe after natural disasters, friends let their friends know they've arrived home in one piece after a night out. Hashtags raise awareness and much-needed cash for disaster relief. YouTube videos warn against our subconscious prejudices, tell inspirational recovery stories, and teach us about blockchain, dart frogs, and how to open wine bottles without a corkscrew. Social media facilitated the Arab Spring, the 2014 Ukrainian Revolution, and the Occupy Movement. It also meant that millions of young people across the world could watch Greta Thunberg's speeches and mobilize their own schools to strike against climate change.

The key lies in making sure that we control the internet, rather than letting it control us. As a parent, this is where it's vital that you step in. If your child is spending hours of the day reflexively scooping their phone out of their pocket and scrolling through it, then it's unlikely they are fully engaging with the world, devoting their full attention to schoolwork, or forming and nurturing real-world relationships. It is unlikely because those three things are not what the companies behind the glowing icons on their iPhones make money from them doing.

But there are things you can turn to for help.

A growing number of tools are being created to help people curb their time spent online. Dumbphones – or phones without internet capabilities – are becoming more prevalent, as people are realizing just how often smartphones hijack their attention. Productivity apps limit the amount of time spent on certain sites, and Yondr pouches make it possible to lock your phone away for a set amount of time.* There are also a growing number of digital detox camps and retreats, like those run by Tanya Goodin's organization, which aims to kick-start the process of rethinking your digital habits.

Tanya Goodin is a digital entrepreneur, founder of the digital detox specialist Time to Log Off, and author of *Stop Staring at Screens*. When I called her to ask what she thought would become of the current crop of internet users, she explained that she was far less worried about Generation Z, or iGen (those born after 1995), than she was about millennials (those born between 1985 and 1994).

'Millennials were sold the idea that the internet would be this great, positive force in their lives,' she said. 'They tried to

---

* As I'm writing, 1,000 British schools have committed to introducing compulsory Yondr pouches for students' phones.

promote themselves as brands, believing that they would all become famous and get deals.'

And this isn't as true for the following generation?

'No, they see it as naff to try and promote yourself like that. They're far more likely to use the internet for speaking privately. Snapchat, WhatsApp, and Instagram DMs are where the real action is happening now.'

The rise of Snapchat has occurred in parallel with a fall in 'traditional' social media use. Where once 66 per cent of twelve-to-fifteen-year-olds used Facebook, the number is now closer to 40 per cent. Twitter and Instagram accounts are increasingly kept private, which means that all followers have to be approved before being allowed to view the posts, which can only be a good thing.

Tanya said that she had recently spoken to a class of four-teen-year-old girls and learned that four of them had already switched to dumbphones after finding their 'smarter' cousins overwhelming and distracting. Other kids had shown similarly impressive methods of self-control, such as swapping phones while revising, that made her hopeful that this generation would be better able to prioritize life over technology.*

I hope that she's right, though it feels difficult not to despair when you're asking children to resist the lure of apps designed specifically by giant companies to eat up as much of their time as possible. Even if they realize too many hours staring at a screen

---

* I found another interesting example of this in the book *Solitude* by Michael Harris, which explores the psychology of being alone. He writes about a group of kids who are tired of being constantly glued to their phones, but also know that their parents expect constant reassurance that they're alive and un-dismembered. To get around this, they would have a designated texter, who would hold all of the phones and text all of the parents while the rest of the friends went gambolling freely through the woods. Really, the woods.

isn't doing them any good, asking them to resist is like suggesting they walk around with pockets full of marshmallows and only take a small nibble of a single piece once a day.

Tanya offered a useful piece of advice that's sat at the back of my mind ever since. When she speaks to children, she asks them to see the difference between active and passive social media use: are you posting in a community board for local Labrador owners or are you scrolling through ten thousand pictures of people with more defined abs than you? Are you participating, or are you being used? Are you gaining something, or are you losing out?

Computers should make our lives more enjoyable and less stressful, rather than being time-sucking black holes financed by advertisers on the other side of the world. But young people need a reason to value their time enough to reclaim it. Maybe the recent upsurge in activism will offer this. Maybe the fight for a better world will involve reshaping the digital landscape to the benefit of a new generation. Maybe you should let young Oscar skip school and stand outside parliament waving a placard that reads 'Climate Change Can Suck My Balls', and not just because the planet needs him, but because he needs a story, a purpose, something that can nudge him into thinking twice the next time he finds himself swirling into a sinkhole of clickbait and *Candy Crush*.

As well as lost time, there are very real worries about the link between mental health troubles and internet use. There is a connection, even if we are being slow to acknowledge and deal with the problem. Part of the difficulty lies in trying to work out whether anxious and depressed teenagers turn to social media more often, or turning to social media more often is making them anxious and depressed. But even if its role in anxiety and depression is not completely clear, it's obvious from research and case studies that internet use is contributing hugely to the epidemic of sleep deprivation, body image problems, and cyberbullying, none of which are particularly beneficial to keeping your head healthy. Young people are unhappier than ever, and I don't think it's wild speculation to lay some of the blame at the feet of the devices designed to hijack their minds.

Don't forget

- The reason your teenager can't put down their phone isn't (necessarily) because they find you boring, it's because every app, site, and notification on it has been designed by committee to hijack their attention.
- Breaking a habit formed over some of the most pivotal years is going to be difficult. Breaking a habit while wandering around with your drug of choice in your pocket is going to be extremely difficult.
- There are a number of ways and means of trying to take back control of internet use, and if you talk to your child about how they feel it's affecting their life, you might be surprised about how willing they are to give some of them a go. Most kids don't cherish the hours they lose to social media, they're just helpless to resist.
- Encourage your teenagers to scrutinize their own internet use. They need to be asking themselves, am I using the

internet, or is the internet using me? Make them aware of how much they're being manipulated by these huge companies; in that way you'll tap into their anti-establishment instincts.

Homework

Although getting locked into Snapstreaks and Instagram likes might take a little time and require a network of friends who also use them, the techniques used by these companies are common to many areas of the digital economy. If you haven't already, maybe because you spent the last few years on the International Space Station or in a prison, try downloading *Candy Crush* or *Gardenscapes* or any of the other brightly coloured, dopamine-triggering mobile games. Play for fifteen minutes and see how difficult it feels to stop.

Lesson Two:

Adolescence is Not an Illness

Mental health in the age of anxiety

I

Growing up, I was regularly told by my mother that under-eighteens needed to be accompanied by a parent when visiting the doctor.

'Why?' I'd ask.

'In case something happens,' my mum would say.

'Like what?'

'Like they try to touch you, or they say you say they tried to touch you because you want to get them in trouble.'

'You have to come in case the doctor's a paedo?'

She would nod. 'Or in case you say they're a paedo.'

This was either a lie or a misunderstanding. There is no rule about parents having to be there in order to prevent inappropriate doctor–patient relations. Not knowing this, I constantly arranged appointments for severe back acne* hoping that at some point my mum would be overwhelmed by a desire to empty her bladder and give me some alone time with the doctor. This never happened.

What did happen was that six seconds of eventual googling proved her ever-present-mum rule to be untrue. I covertly made my own appointment at the age of sixteen.

By that point, I had probably read ten books' worth of online material about various mental illnesses. Any original ways I had of expressing how I felt had been long subsumed by psychological jargon. Unipolar, bipolar, alexithymia, neurosis, autonomic arousal, derealization, depersonalization: I had a list of more symptoms than I knew what to do with.

As a result, it was impossible to tell what was being felt and what I felt I was supposed to feel. What started as a relief – ah, that's what this is – became a crutch. I am depressed, so I am not getting out of bed or going to school or eating anything that isn't equal parts sugar and palm oil.

The doctor didn't know any of this when I sat opposite him. I didn't fully understand any of this. I knew only that I felt terrible and wanted to be taken very seriously.

'What seems to be the problem?' the doctor asked.

'I feel depressed,' I announced. 'And anxious.'

'Okay.'

---

* Known in common parlance as 'bacne', an embarrassing ailment that leaves your school shirts looking like scattergraphs.

'Also, I'm suffering from hypersomnia.'

A raised eyebrow.

'That means I'm sleeping a lot,' I explained, patiently.

'I know what it means.'

'And I've been experiencing panic attacks and bouts of extreme hopelessness.'

'I see. How would you like me to help? Antidepressants?'

I blinked.

Was this a trap? Or a joke? Are doctors allowed to be sarcastic?

'Yes.'

'Do you have one in mind?'

'Fluoxetine?'

'A good first choice, I'm on them myself.' He narrowed his eyes, squinting at his computer screen. 'I see here you have two suicide attempts listed.'

'Guilty.'

'Do you still have suicidal thoughts or feelings?'

'No.'

'Because I have to warn you that fluoxetine can cause suicidal thoughts and feelings.'

'Really?'

'Yes, but very rarely.'

'Okay.'

'Great.'

'Fantastic.'

'Brilliant.'

That was the extent of the consultation.

I bounced out of the surgery with a prescription for what the

Americans call Prozac, perfectly convinced that the future would be a bright and beautiful place. It was not.

Reading over the dialogue above, I understand that it sounds unlikely. Would a doctor really ask a sixteen-year-old patient what drug they wanted to be prescribed? Would they really admit that whatever ailment we were dealing with was so little understood that my guess was as good as theirs? But that was exactly what he said: 'Do you have one in mind?' Do you have in mind the name of a pill you might like to take that will significantly alter your brain chemistry at an age when the wet meat harbouring the seeds of your personality is still taking shape?

Of course I do! I read about it on the internet!

In retrospect, it's possible that my mum should have been present.

II

The internet didn't just alert me to potential cures for depression, it quite likely played a role in causing it as well. But it's a difficult thing to pin down. Studies that find connections between the two typically run up against the same problem: are mentally ill kids retreating into the internet, or is the internet provoking mental illness in them?

A 2019 study conducted by Johns Hopkins Bloomberg School of Public Health tried to make the leap from correlation to cause by taking into account the pre-existing mental health problems of participants in the year before their research. They followed

6,000 kids aged twelve to fifteen and found that those who used social media for over three hours a day were twice as likely to develop mental health problems as their unplugged counterparts. The set-up of the study suggested that it was more than likely internet use triggers mental health issues, rather than the other way around.

The internet being damaging is not a revelation. You probably feel instinctively that it's not healthy for your child to spend so much time staring at a screen, even without knowing what's going on behind it. It's easy to come up with a list of potential ways the internet might cause emotional harm: cyberbullying, heightened self-consciousness, exposure to damaging content, wasting time, missing out on real-world experiences, substituting actual friendships for virtual ones. Almost every under-eighteen I spoke to said they could connect instances of depression to internet binges. 'It's like, yeah, I know it's making me down or whatever,' said Rory, 'but, I don't know. What else am I going to do?' Nobody seems to be particularly infatuated with the internet, it's just something that's there. The internet is like the bowl of Celebrations in an office kitchen: you know you shouldn't eat them, but you can see them, they're there, so you eat one. And then another. And another.

Without meaning to, kids find themselves drawn into their phones or computers for hours at a time. These internet binges are almost always followed by a kind of hollow, disappointed confusion. Where has that time gone? What have I done? There is none of the satisfaction of having followed the arc of a story or levelled up on a game, just a bizarre sense of having been duped out of a few hours. I still feel a kind of dull ache when I remember days on which I woke up wide-eyed with plans for writing stories, going over and above with school projects, composing music, reading books, or painting, and ended the same days having done exactly none of those things because I got sucked into the computer screen. The internet has a peculiar way of making you forget what it is that's really important to you.

A 2007 UNICEF study of happiness in twenty-one economically developed countries ranked Britain's young people last. But what is it they have to be so unhappy about? you might be asking. They have computers and phones and those hoverboards that don't really hover. Everyone's too afraid of legal repercussions to smack them when they mess up. They all get medals for participation and spend art lessons drawing their feelings. There's no war, no typhus, no miners' strike or poll tax or fears of imminent nuclear Armageddon.

Shouldn't they be bouncing off the walls?

Where is this unhappiness coming from? A quick look over the numerous articles on the subject will flag up a number of common suggestions:

- Exam pressure
- Poverty
- Bullying
- Problems at home
- Body image issues
- Health problems
- Social media

The thing that jumps out is that only one of these is a recent phenomenon, and that recent phenomenon directly amplifies at least three of the other issues. The internet, most notably social media, is occupying a central role in the lives of young people and changing how they perceive themselves and the world around them.

Studies that randomly assign groups to delete Facebook for four weeks find that, after those four weeks are up, these groups feel notably less depressed and lonely. However, similar studies also showed that people who used social media very moderately were slightly happier than those who didn't use it at all. This likely means there is an optimal level of usage that prevents young people from feeling left out while also making sure they're not susceptible to the harmful effects. The 'safe' level seems to be around half an hour per day. I have met and spoken to exactly zero young people whose social media use falls into this goldilocks zone. As we've covered, most apps and sites are built to hook users into using them for as long as possible. We are essentially giving children bottles of vodka and asking them to drink responsibly. Just a sip, we say. I know it's addictive, but any more than that is bad for you.

One theory about why social media may make teenagers unhappy, as put forward by Amy Ellis Nutt and Frances Jensen in the book *The Teenage Brain*, involves a hormone called THP. In adults, this is like the glass of wine your brain treats itself to after a shitty day. You become stressed, your brain releases THP, you become less stressed. In teenagers, however, THP does the opposite. Rather than drinking a glass of wine, it is like eating a shit sandwich at the end of a shitty day. They get stressed, THP spurts out, and they get more stressed. Social media increases stress, and stress in teenagers increases stress, so it follows that time spent on computers isn't exactly going to help them unwind.

If social media doesn't make people happy, what does?

Possibly the most famous study on happiness is a Harvard study that has tracked 286 men from the university from 1938 onwards, as they grew up, grew old, fell in and out of love, had children, promotions, health scares, and existential panic attacks. After eighty years, only nine were left alive. The project continued by following their children.

The results of the study came as a surprise.

More than genetics or wealth or IQ or any other variable, it was the quality of relationships that seemed to predict how happy the Harvard alumni reported being. This meant not just how many friends a participant had, but whether these were the kinds of friends you tolerated during football matches or talked to for hours about how anxious the thought of becoming a parent made you. Did they have people they could confide in about their fears for the end of the world? Did they have people who genuinely shared in their joys and sorrows?

This is relevant to the internet when you realize that what most teens think of as socializing seems to have few of the mental health benefits of face-to-face interaction. The internet will never offer them the same feelings of euphoria and giddiness that doing stupid things with friends will – the stuff of memories you recall and laugh about when you're older – because they are not participating in anything tangible. We are built to socialize physically, to read body language, trade expressions, and exist beside each other while we offload our grievances, anxieties, and bad jokes. Maybe, online, your child might help propagate a meme or express outrage, but once pictures flash up of Keegan and Milo on a beach, the despair of being alone and tapping at a phone in the gloom of their bedroom sinks in. It's difficult to imagine a reunion at which drunk alumni reminisce about Snapchat messages or Facebook posts. These tools, which should enable people to get together more easily, end up replacing actual hanging out with an unsatisfying, algorithm-driven imposter. They are a convenient, habit-forming, and sustenance-free replacement for a vital component of healthy mental life.

This ties in neatly with the conclusions reached by Johann Hari in his seminal book *Lost Connections*. Here he argues that most mental illnesses are not the result of our brains going wrong, but of our lives going wrong in one way or another. He looks at cases of people diagnosed with 'endogenous' depression, or depression that arises without any apparent outside cause, and sees that most suffered some kind of emotional trauma in the year leading up to their diagnosis or were living lives that left them disconnected from the environment, themselves, or other people. It's an idea corroborated by the World Health Organization, who, as far back as 2011, said 'Mental health is produced socially: the presence or absence of mental health is above all a social indicator and therefore requires social, as well as individual, solutions.'

Hari himself took an SSRI* for years without any apparent

---

* Selective Serotonin reuptake inhibitor. The most popular breed of antidepressants. Fluoxetine (Prozac) being the most famous member of the family.

benefit. It was only when he started questioning why he wasn't getting any better and after picking apart hundreds of studies that he discovered how unlikely these medications were to help us. Instead, he claims, most mental illnesses arise from or are triggered by disconnection in our day-to-day lives. We do not live in close communities, we do not generally work meaningful jobs, most of us are not free to spend long periods of time in nature. We are, for the most part, shut away in our homes, trying to relax after days spent doing things we're not wired to do. And who is most likely to be indoors staring into a shoddy simulation of community?

It doesn't seem like a mad leap to wonder whether young people are struggling to form meaningful relationships in an age when many of their relationships are being shaped and monetized by Silicon Valley billionaires. Social media isn't designed to facilitate deep relationships; it is designed to keep you coming back by offering the illusion of popularity and interconnectedness. In 2017, almost half of young people in the UK reported feeling lonely some or most of the time, despite the fact that they are permanently wired into systems that purport to keep them connected. Somehow, snapchatting each other endless pictures of coffee mugs superimposed with 'your mum smells like a cinema' is not fulfilling the need they have for human connection. Loneliness is also not just a moment of missing out, but a persistent, pernicious sense of disconnection that has been shown to be harmful not only to mental but to physical health. A 2015 study by Holt-Lunstad et al. equated the health impact of loneliness with smoking fifteen cigarettes a day. And while we associate chronic loneliness with the elderly, for a generation who are not necessarily getting as much practice at socializing as their ancestors, it might be something they become inclined to fall into.

I both smoke fifteen cigarettes a day and often feel lonely. This, I assume, means my life expectancy is roughly the same as that of a Soviet space dog. And this is at least partly down to having spent my formative years nurturing online relationships rather than real-world ones. I'm very grateful to have stumbled into an internet community at a time when I felt lonelier than ever but I also appreciate that, however much I wanted them to, friends on the internet were never going to be an adequate substitution for a real-world support network.

Now, instead of a close circle of friends, I find myself an adult with close to a hundred people whose emails I still feel obliged to reply to. And I can feel, acutely, the ramifications this has for mental health. What do you do with your thoughts and feelings when you have no one to share them with? You either get a therapist or express them on the internet, I suppose, neither of which are the healthy, reciprocal relationships we probably need most of all.

Mental health disorders are not simply unhappiness, but the two are inextricably linked. Poor mental health generally leads to unhappiness and unhappiness is more than capable of triggering certain mental health conditions.

Whether or not the mental health crisis is caused by unhappiness or unhappiness is caused by the mental health crisis, it's clear that many of the people who need help most aren't getting

it. Mental health problems constitute 23 per cent of the disease burden but only receive 13 per cent of the NHS budget.
Seventy per cent of young people with identifiable mental health
problems do not get help sufficiently early. Waiting times are
incredibly long. Access to specialist help is difficult to come by.
If you put your hand up and admit you're being trailed by rain
clouds, you're more likely to be given an antidepressant menu
than an opportunity to speak with a qualified counsellor. And
this is true the world over. Therapeutic treatment is expensive
and time-consuming compared to medication. As vital as pills
can be in certain cases, they are never a cure, only a way of
managing symptoms. Around 80 per cent of people prescribed
antidepressants stop taking them within a month. I'm not surprised. In fact, I imagine this is for the best.

III

Navigating mental health as a teen might be so difficult partly
because the symptoms of being an adolescent can be so similar
to the symptoms of being depressed or clinically anxious:

- Antisocial behaviour
- Poor impulse control
- Sleeping too much
- Not sleeping enough
- Increased anxiety
- Mood swings

- Withdrawal
- A reduction in physical movement
- Feelings of worthlessness

You'll find these listed under the diagnostic criteria for major depression, and you'll also find them in most fifteen-year-olds. At that age, I very rarely left my bedroom, would regularly drink to blackout, either slept for three hours or thirteen hours a night, communicated mostly through shouting, smirking, or crying, and spent every spare moment lying flat on my back with a laptop open on my chest. Tick, tick, tick, tick, tick.

No parent wants their child to be reclusive and surly, but when does it cross from normal teenage growing pains to something more serious? Should a teenager ever feel 'worthless'? Can such feelings be eliminated? Should we try to eliminate them? All of them? So that a young person grows up never doubting any aspect of themselves?

There are a host of clear neurological reasons why teenagers become unrecognizable compared to the children they once were. For the first time, sex hormones which have lain dormant since birth are unleashed on the body. Underdeveloped frontal lobes are faced with unfamiliar situations and emotions. Synapses are pruned like bonsai trees. And the amygdala is relied upon far too heavily for a region of the brain concerned with emotion and survival, rather than logic or reason.

'Oscar used to be charming and sweet! He used to put on plays for us! He used to help me bake, hug his dad, and play with his sister! And now? Now he only sits in his room, morosely

itching his ball-sack and calling people he's never met knobgob-
blers through an Xbox headset. It's not fair!'

Maybe not, but adolescence has no known cure. At least it's
only temporary. The problem is separating normal teenage struggles from the kind that might require medical intervention. When
does staying in your room become social isolation? Oversleeping
turn into hypersomnia? Or insecurity about how big your nose
looks on Instagram morph into truly damaging feelings of inadequacy? There are no concrete answers to any of these questions.
Most of the literature I've read seems to say things are a problem
when they 'interfere with your ability to engage in day-to-day life'.
But if day-to-day life involves spending eight hours a day in an
ugly building with people you don't like, then I'd counter that
you'd need something wrong with your head if you do want to
engage with it. Ultimately, what is manageable and what is not
is something that can only be worked out between a parent and
their child. There is no line in the sand with mental illness on one
side and day-to-day upset on the other. There are just different
people facing different trials.

Like many teenagers, I refused to see myself as anything
other than an adult who, for some bizarre reason, hadn't yet
been granted the privileges of adulthood. I was convinced my
romances were unparalleled, my existential thoughts unrivalled,
and my low moods unlike anything any other human had ever
suffered through. Helpful, then, to be aware that there was a
proper medical name for this tragic unhappiness: depression. It
never occurred to me that the feelings I felt might be anything
other than extraordinary.

(This ability to see diagnosable mental illness where it might not be necessary seems to be common amongst adolescents: a 2017 NHS survey conducted using GP data found that self-reported incidents of mental health disorders amongst young people increased six-fold between 1999 and 2014, while researchers could find no equivalent rise in those who had been given actual psychiatric assessments.)

I'm not saying that I didn't have any diagnosable symptoms of mental illness, just that I was painfully overzealous in reaching verdicts on what those symptoms meant. I revelled in self-diagnosis (this kind of internet-induced hypochondria is now so prevalent it has its own name: cyberchondria). Sticking polysyllabic labels onto things made them serious and indisputable – serious and indisputable being two things most teenagers long to be. If I had been able to find any mention of it online, I would have happily diagnosed myself with spontaneous-darkening-penis syndrome. I wanted to be able to label my feelings as diseases. Diseases could be cured, feelings could only be felt. Illnesses were palpable problems, emotions were just dull things that every other dumbass had to reckon with. I was convinced I was suffering from:

- **Depression:** Because I thought about death a lot, couldn't sleep, and never wanted to do anything.
- **Bipolar:** Because I often changed my mind, couldn't sleep, and sometimes wanted to do lots of things.
- **Borderline Personality Disorder:** Because I liked the film *Girl, Interrupted* starring Winona Ryder and Angelina

Jolie, and imagined I would find a lot of like-minded friends while interred in a psychiatric hospital.

- **Schizophrenia:** Because I believed, to an embarrassingly late age, in my own magical abilities. This included but was not limited to: control of the weather, control of TV characters, the ability to travel in time, and the skill of funnelling bodily energy into glowing orbs called 'psi balls'.
- **Narcissistic personality disorder:** Because I wanted everyone to like me but I didn't like very many people.
- **Anxiety disorder:** Because I worried a lot, at least partially about whether or not I had the disorders listed above.

It might sound extreme, but think about every time you've freaked out over a lump, bump, mole or cold sore because it might spell cancer. As soon as you feel an unexpected swelling, your mind jumps to weeping relatives, robotic beds, painful bouts of fruitless chemotherapy. You've had the importance of fondling your genitals for unexpected developments drummed into you so profoundly – and quite rightly, of course – that you are probably unable to come across a skin tag without thinking you have three months to live. This fear might save your life; it might also cause a fair bit of anxiety.

In the same way, if kids have mental health ideas clumsily pushed on them, it's kind of understandable that they might start identifying normal low moods as depressions, nervousness as anxiety, and introversion as antisocial behaviour. And what will the consequences of that be? When I spoke to Erica, Simon, and

Samson, all three claimed a version of being depressed 'maybe a couple of hours a week'. This is not only not possible, but not in the least bit helpful. A kid who believes he has the disease of depression is probably going to find himself feeling more depressed. It's not a hugely uplifting belief to hold about yourself. It is, however, one that's difficult to shake once it's gained a foothold.

I don't think we shouldn't teach young people about the importance of mental health and asking for support when you need it, but we need to be careful about the way things are framed. You shape the lens through which teenagers see themselves when you introduce them to ideas like 'depression' and 'anxiety disorder'. The lessons around these should involve more than box ticking. They should be nuanced, in depth, and cover a range of perspectives and possibilities. We cannot just tell young people: here is what depression is, please tell us if you have it. We also cannot afford to let them spend hours at computers diagnosing themselves. They will not do a good job of it. No one does a good job of it.

Medical student syndrome is the name given to the phenomenon of medical students becoming convinced that they're suffering from the diseases they're studying. They douse crabby pubes with acid and start feeling their own genitals itch. They lance buboes and sense swellings under their own skins. They administer speed to narcoleptics and begin noticing that they too become incredibly drowsy after their mid-morning Snickers.

I learned this from drunkenly watching an episode of *Scrubs* on a plane and went on to find out that two researchers, Howes and Salkovskis, found that between 70 and 80 per cent of medical students have suffered from the condition at some point. If medical students who ought to know better frequently start hallucinating physical symptoms, what chance does a kid alone at his computer have of understanding his own mental state? At a time when the internet has led many of us to become our own triage nurses, how will this affect the ability of actual professionals to diagnose us, especially with disorders that have no symptoms but the feelings we tell them about?

There are virtually no physical tests for any mental illnesses. All that GPs, psychologists, and psychiatrists have to go on is what we describe. If, hypothetically, you're a kid who loves drugs, as I was, and you've heard of a pill that makes you happy, as I did, it isn't going to take much homework to memorize a list of symptoms that'll get you the pill you want, even if you're going to be hugely disappointed by its effects. I'm not saying all kids are faking mental illnesses to get prescribed antidepressants, but I'm saying the thought crossed my mind. Okay, it more than crossed my mind. Not for antidepressants, which were easy to obtain, but for amphetamines, or the purer form of the speed I sometimes took because it was a third of the price of a gram of anything else.

When I learned that powerful amphetamines were prescribed for ADHD, I memorized a few of the symptoms, booked a consultation, and began furiously bouncing my leg up and down as I sat down in the doctor's office.

'What seems to be the problem?' he said.

(This was a different doctor from the one who'd prescribed

fluoxetine. He was older and more serious looking and I wanted my other, depressed doctor back.)

'I can't concentrate,' I said. 'I have a very short attention span and get bored easily.'

'Is that so?'

'I also talk too much and fidget relentlessly.'

'I can see your leg is moving an awful lot.'

'I'm always like this.'

He squinted at his computer. 'It says here you're on fluoxetine. As you may or may not be aware, restlessness is a possible side effect of certain SSRIs. Have you tried citalopram?'

I panicked. 'It can't be fluoxetine,' I told him. 'I stopped taking it months ago.'

He beamed, as though the case had been solved. 'In that case,' he said. 'I recommend you start taking it again.'

And thus ended my quest for amphetamines.

But beyond possibilities of self-fulfilling prophecy and manipulation, mental health diagnoses themselves are far from scientific. They change with each edition of the *DSM** that comes out and may well, if past trends are anything to go by, begin popping in and out of existence, splitting into separate ailments, and merging with others as time goes by. Homosexuality was listed as a disorder until 1973. Gender identity disorder disappeared in 2013.

---

* The *Diagnostic and Statistical Manual of Mental Disorders*. Sometimes called the bible of psychiatry. Slightly less boring than the Bible, thanks to the inclusion of ailments such as clinical lycanthropy (where someone believes they have, do, or will turn into an animal) koro (where you are convinced your penis is shrinking) and hoarding disorder (as made famous by cheap reality TV).

In 1994, alcoholism split into alcohol abuse and alcohol dependence, only to merge again into alcohol use disorder come 2013. These mental illnesses are not decided by scientific research but by committee. They are not immovable monuments by which we can judge ourselves. They are likely to change as society does.

From the fourteenth century onwards, there were huge numbers of recorded cases of people worried that their heads and hearts were made of glass and liable to shatter at any moment. King Charles VI spent whole days motionless in bed, swaddled in blankets in case his organs smashed like dropped wineglasses. By the nineteenth century, the glass delusion was almost non-existent. In contrast, as reality TV conquers our screens today, cases of 'Truman Show syndrome' abound, in which people become convinced that their lives are being broadcast for the entire world to see. As newspapers stoke our darkest fears, and true-crime podcasts accompany us on even the briefest walks, levels of anxiety rise.

IV

As someone who is absolutely not a parent, I imagine that having kids must involve finding a balance between keeping them safe and keeping them from living in constant terror. Both perception and expectation shape mental illnesses. Mental illnesses can not only reflect our internal states but the world around us. What does this mean for how we talk about mental health to young people? I'm not sure, but if I tell you there are monsters roaming your neighbourhood, it's quite likely you'll start hearing them at night. And if I tell you there are bugs under your skin, you might very well get itchy.

There's a joke in Judd Apatow's recent stand-up special in which he recalls an argument with his daughter about the kinds of photos she's been posting on her Instagram. He tells her she can't keep posting pictures showing skin, that it's inappropriate. She's confused.

'You can't put up a picture of you in a bikini on a beach on Instagram,' he insists.

'Why?' she wants to know. 'People on the beach saw me in a bikini on the beach.'

He tells her again it's inappropriate.

'But why?' she wants to know. 'What's going to happen? What'll happen if I put the pictures up? What is going to happen? Tell me!'

He pauses.

'It's fine,' he sighs. 'You're adorable, don't worry about it.'

We want to keep kids safe; we don't necessarily want them to know the exact details of what they're being kept safe from. We introduce them to certain ideas when they're suitably mature. At the age of ten we might teach them about safe boundaries, but not about how exactly the daddy's willy goes into the mummy's fanny. In the same way, we can teach kids the tools and behaviours that it appears may prevent certain mental illnesses, without giving them black dogs and bogeymen to cower from. We can, however, only do this if we steer away from certain prevalent ideas about what exactly mental illness is. Unfortunately, these are ideas that almost all teenagers now hold.

It's become obvious to me just how much psychiatric language has infiltrated the vocabulary of youth – even more so than when I was sixteen. While interviewing them for this book, Ellis casually mentioned 'cyclical thinking', Erica brought up 'unipolar depression' and Simon, Reese, and Tom could all name three antidepressants despite never having been prescribed them. These are only a few examples. There has been a shift from the near-denial of certain mental illnesses by the majority of one generation, to an all-out embracing of them by the next. Young people are clued up. They are quickest to point out that OCD isn't just liking your trainers clean, depression isn't just sadness, and schizophrenia isn't when you're sometimes Nice Barbara and sometimes Angry Barbara.

While adults talk about the need to destigmatize mental health, kids are more than happy to compare their prescriptions. For many, especially those in bigger cities, the stigma never existed. Even when I was younger, this was a conversation I repeatedly heard variations on:

'Yeah, I just switched to citalopram.'

'How much?'

'Forty mil.'

'I switched to that and it stopped working. Now I'm on paroxetine.'

'That gave me headaches.'

'It made Ross Brickwater want to jump off the motorway bridge.'

'Really?'

'Apparently.'

ADOLESCENCE IS NOT AN ILLNESS

As with self-harm, I don't think this is born entirely out of thinking prescription drugs are some kind of badge of honour – although this is an idea that a few teenagers put to me – but the idea that being mentally unwell is now fashionable is something kids seem to embrace.

Turning on the TV or opening a magazine, the overriding message is that a person isn't worth anything unless they've suffered. From TV talent shows to actors doing press junkets, everyone is expected to air their trauma in order to prove they're worthy of success. People on pedestals are not supposed to have stepped gracefully onto them, they're supposed to have scrabbled up, skinning their knees while being fiercely clawed at by an army of demons. The once-mocked sob stories of *X Factor* contestants are now expected of everyone. If you have not experienced great pain or hardship, you ought to surrender your place in the world to someone who has.

There is something wonderful in the impulse to lift up those who have suffered. There is also something deeply disturbing in watching people try to outbid each other with the level of pain they've endured. Like the four Yorkshiremen sketch by Monty Python, in which the cast try to outdo each other with how much hardship they endured growing up, eventually devolving into Eric Idle proclaiming that he had to 'get up in the morning at ten o'clock at night, half an hour before I went to bed, drink a cup of sulphuric acid, work twenty-nine hours a day down the mill, and pay the mill owner for permission to come to work, and when we got home, our dad and our mother would kill us, and dance about on our graves singing "Hallelujah".'

Medication fits into this because taking medicine implies you are genuinely unwell. Look, it says, this is a real illness, and I am taking real pills for it. In many circles, mental illness can still feel like a thing that is in doubt, something that needs proof, so we cling on to diagnoses to show that we aren't being overly sensitive, lazy, or antisocial. I sometimes find it hard to understand what the fifteen-year-old me was up to, but in this case I can see it clearly: he wanted drugs and he wanted to be taken seriously. He wanted to know he had a thing called depression. Having achieved this diagnosis, he could relax into it, he could wear it comfortably as armour against anyone who doubted that he felt much worse than they did.

The self-awareness that this knowledge has endowed young people with is a huge step forward. It should mean that teenagers are more ready to seek help, receive help, and, ultimately, recover.

But it doesn't.

I don't think teenagers taking notice of their own emotional states is in any way a bad thing; what I do worry about is the lens through which they see them. Every young person I spoke to saw depression and anxiety in terms of what is known in psychiatry as 'the biomedical model'. This is the idea that illnesses like depression are simply the result of malfunctioning brains. They are not caused by shitty life experiences, chaotic childhoods, discrimination, poverty, or anything other than something going spontaneously wrong in the mechanisms of the brain. For example, maybe your head just doesn't produce as much serotonin as it ought to, and for that reason you feel less happy than you should, and this is what we label depression. The logical fix for this is a pill that helps keep more serotonin floating about between your synapses. You take the pill, and you'll be fixed. It's as simple as treating diarrhoea, yeast infections, or scurvy.

Up until fairly recently I unquestioningly believed this. It's why I took pills. It's why I believed I'd be at the mercy of some brand of psychiatric disease until the sweet release of death. But you don't have to wade far into critical reading to see how little water the idea really holds. If mental illness is just a glitch in your grey matter, then why can we so clearly tie childhood trauma to most disorders? Why are rates of mental illness higher in immigrants, minorities, and those living in poverty? Why have we, for no apparent reason, found ourselves dealing with a generation of young people who seem more depressed and anxious that their predecessors? Are they just incredibly unlucky? Were half of the new brains to arrive on earth post-1990 somehow faulty?

Most critics point their fingers at the American pharmaceutical industry to explain why the biomedical model has taken root in our imaginations. Drug companies sponsored trials that invariably suggested their products could lead to improved quality of life for those suffering from ailments of the brain. It sounded wonderful and, if pills solved the problem, how could mental illness be the result of anything other than a broken-down brain? The cause of most mental illnesses, these studies seemed to suggest, was that these people were not consuming the products on offer from these pharmaceutical companies.

Whether this started across the Atlantic or not, the NHS is now doling out seventy-five million antidepressants a year. We are as much in the grip of psychiatric medication as our smiley transatlantic cousins. Why? Because in many ways, it's simpler to understand mental health in these terms. As Nathan Filer says in his wonderful book *The Heartland: Finding and Losing Schizophrenia*: 'Better it be understood that a young millennial who's falling apart while struggling to pay two thirds of their increasingly precarious salary to rent a mouldy room in a shared house is suffering from "panic disorder" than countenance the possibility that the real sickness is located elsewhere.' Because of course it's easier to dole out mild sedatives, with little to no benefit, than it is to try and reorganize a crumpled economy or level an unequal society. And young people happily accept the idea too, because it's directly contravenes the views their parents may hold on mental illness while legitimizing the concerns they have about themselves. The preceding generations struggled to view mental health issues as tangible ailments. The current generations struggle to see them as anything more complex than a broken leg. In seeking to legitimize mental illness this way, you inadvertently reduce it. You reduce it to such a degree that it becomes untreatable. If depression, for example, was a result purely of low serotonin, then SSRIs would work for us all and we would no longer have the problem to reckon with. This is not the case, and if the only tools we turn to are chemical, we are never going to find any meaningful or effective treatment for those who need it most. Why would we bother to talk about our feelings or the things that cause us pain if we understand chronic unhappiness as purely chemical? Will kids really be more likely to be open about what is weighing on them if they believe that the sole cause of their despair is a malfunctioning head?

I was thrilled to read that depression was an illness of the brain. Finally, I had an answer for why I felt like a bag of dog shit left out in the rain. A scrap of paper torn out of the *New Scientist* made the perfect middle finger up to Mum. Look, I could say, it's a real actual disease in my body! Fuck you! You're wrong! She didn't listen, of course, but that didn't matter. What mattered was that I had an illness and the illness had a cure.

V

After being told by one psychiatrist I was bipolar rather than just depressed, I began carrying this diagnosis around with conviction. It shaped how I saw myself and what I thought I was capable of. I did not go to university. Instead, I started drinking the days through. I also continued taking various psychiatric medications, never questioning the need to do so.

I was convinced that I was physically ill and therefore needed to be medicated, like the tens of thousands of other under-eighteens in the UK. I would not lead a functioning life like my hair-gelled, sports-obsessed classmates. I would, inevitably, sink.

There can be a real place and need for psychiatric medication. It can make life bearable, it can make life better, it can prevent suicides, self-injury, and harm to others. For certain mental illnesses, including many psychotic disorders, it can be the most effective treatment. However, I've known two family members who were prescribed Prozac after people near to them died. They went and told their doctors: a person I loved has died and now I feel sad, and they were given a tablet to straighten that out. Is grief really a problem in need of a solution? Clearly not. It's as much a part of being human as laughter, nightmares, and bellybutton fluff, and trying to diminish it will be neither successful nor productive. And grief isn't the only normal element of life or being human that we seem increasingly determined to medicate against.

Adolescence is not an illness. Mood swings and reckless behaviour are intrinsic parts of growing up, with a clear basis in the fact that while you're growing, your brain is still developing. If we lean towards the American model of medicalizing every aspect of life and personality, we are going to end up doing serious damage to our kids. And if those kids embrace the American model too, they're going to lose any power they have to change their lives for the better.

You can't fix everything with medication, and the rush to do so can end up making things far worse. Side effects are unpredictable, and withdrawal once the medication is stopped can also be severe. But worse than that, taking psychiatric medication also means living in an altered state that not even the foremost researchers completely understand. To live in this altered state at an age when your brain is still developing seems terrifying. We have no idea how antidepressants operate, let alone what they'll do to the swelling grey matter of a kid who still thinks the fridge fills itself. Putting kids on any kind of psychiatric medication is not restoring some natural balance to their brain, it is introducing an intoxicating substance to them on a daily basis.

There are people for whom meds prove life-saving. There are other people for whom they will be entirely unnecessary, but they will keep taking them regardless, because a doctor has told them to do so. This hypothetical doctor will not be incompetent; he'll probably be fearful and overstretched. Nobody wants to be haunted by hanged teenagers. Far better to give them the pills they've read about on the internet.

For the most part, I found the majority of medications I took introduced upsetting side effects without tackling the true problems in any real way. Thinking while under their influence felt like the difference between doing star jumps on land and star jumps in the water. And I would still be prone to periods of not moving from bed, not washing, chain-smoking, drinking, and fist-fighting with the bedroom walls. I did not pause at any point to check whether the medication was making me any happier. In the odd moment I may have reflected that I wasn't particularly joyful, but I'd always get around that by assuring myself that I'd be markedly more unhappy without chemical help.

The scariest amongst them was olanzapine, an antipsychotic used in the treatment of bipolar, which left me feeling like I'd been possessed by a ghost so boring that the world had forgotten him entirely.

The Hamilton Scale is used by mental health workers to grade depression. It goes from the ecstatically happy 0 to stabbing yourself in the heart 51. When Professor Irving Kirsch of Harvard analysed the trials run on antidepressants, they seemed to show an average improvement of 1.8* on the Hamilton Scale. Getting better sleep showed an average improvement of 6 points. Sleep also has the added advantage of not requiring a black box label that dutifully informs you it may cause thoughts of suicide. Though critics will argue that the truly depressed and anxious cannot get better sleep exactly because they are depressed and anxious, I find it hard to believe that every fifteen-year-old who's down to six hours of sleep a night is sleepless with despair, rather than messaging other still-awake friends, trawling through social media, or finding themselves immersed in some purposely addictive game or app.

VI

So young people are embracing the diagnostic model of mental illness, but what's the use of giving these illnesses names if it isn't helping recovery? I'm sure it didn't help me and, if the figures are anything to go by, it isn't helping many other teenagers either. It seems like common sense that talking more about mental illness,

---

* Depending on who you listen to, the finding that antidepressants have a very slight positive benefit is either the result of biased studies, too small to warrant the possible side effects, or a brilliant tool for treating the depressed. The studies were also done on adults. For adolescents and children, a comprehensive 2016 *Lancet Psychiatry* review found that there is no proof that any antidepressant is at all effective for treating depression, with the possible exception of fluoxetine, which may have a very slight effect, although, according to Dr Jon Jureidini, who oversaw the study, the potential benefit is nowhere near big enough to justify the potential harm to developing brains.

teaching its fundamentals to kids, and trying to create an environment in which no one feels afraid to be honest about how they're feeling ought to improve things. So why isn't it working?

Many researchers are increasingly turning away from not only the biomedical, but the diagnostic model of mental illness altogether. How helpful is it to classify a person as having a thing called 'depression' and to treat them the way you treat other people who have a thing called 'depression'? Well, slightly useful, in some cases, is the answer. But it also has the potential to do harm.

Self-fulfilling prophecy has been proven again and again to have a massive impact on young people. They do studies on it all the time. The studies generally go like this:

A group of students are given tests and their scores are recorded. They're then randomly split into two groups and allocated to teachers. One of the teachers is told: your children are the idiot ones. The other teacher is told: your children are the smart ones. In reality, both groups are an equal mix of high-scorers and low-scorers.

After a period of time, the students are all tested again. Invariably, the ones under the tutelage of the teacher who thought they were geniuses improve dramatically, to such a degree that it seems like they actually were all the bright ones all along. Not only that, but the ones whose teacher thought they were morons all scored worse than they had initially.

(Apparently, this was first discovered when the mix-up happened for real in a British school.)

It's a scary finding that ought to have implications for how we arrange our school systems.

Ought to, but doesn't.

We still divide kids into schools and sets based on their abilities at the age of eleven, then scratch our heads when those labelled 'stupid' fail to succeed.*

In psychology, they go on to split the forms of self-fulfilling prophecy into three branches, which I'm writing about now because they all have very cool names that I am reserving for my eventual children:

- **The Pygmalion Effect:** the idea that the higher a teacher's expectations of children, the better their outcomes will be.
- **The Golem Effect:** the idea that the lower a teacher's expectations of children, the worse they're outcomes will be.
- **The Galatea Effect:** the idea that a person's expectations of themselves affect how things turn out.

Clearly, these fit quite easily into ideas about mental health. I find it hard not to think that, in my case, accepting a diagnosis meant accepting decreased expectations for the future. I also find it hard not to think that parents or teachers who are told a certain child is mentally ill might subconsciously (or consciously) treat them in a way that negatively affects their chances of success. As I experienced, there are psychological repercussions: by accepting

---

* I understand that this isn't really related to the topic at hand. I'm sorry. I just wanted to say it.

the illness as purely biological, you surrender your power to do anything about it.

Young people are very quick to believe what they are told about themselves. If a child is told they're worthless, this can take a lifetime to get over. If a person believes they don't deserve to be happy, they will grow up seeking out the unhappiness they believe they deserve.

There is an increasing readiness to accept diagnoses in the case of mental illness, which can mean seeking simplicity where there is none. Depression is not one thing any more than 'a cut' is one thing, and there are so many different shades and depths to it that trying to fit it into a pre-existing framework can be a pointless exercise. Of course, mental illness should be afforded the same level of seriousness as physical illness, but that doesn't mean it will be as simple to diagnose and treat.

VII

When I tried to tell my parents I was 'depressed, or something', they laughed. What do you have to be depressed about? If we were farmers in Uganda, then would you be depressed? Would you be depressed if you were a chimney sweep? You're not depressed, you're lazy and you want attention.

I don't doubt that I was both lazy and attention-seeking. I also don't doubt that this response was harmful. You turn inwards when you're not taken seriously. You shut down. Rather than learning to ask for help, you learn to look for things that will confirm your pain. You want to prove to yourself that you're unwell, that you'd feel the same way even if you were tearing cassava out of the ground in sub-Saharan Africa.

Tom and Ellis, two kids from smaller towns in central England, both told me they don't and won't voice mental health concerns for fear of being belittled or disbelieved. Which is sad, but they were the only two. It seems we have come on fairly quickly in encouraging young people to be honest about their emotional concerns. After a number of years in which every dementedly sincere celebrity gardener and ex-footballer on TV has been mumbling that we ought to 'destigmatize talking about mental health', we are starting to destigmatize talking about mental health, which doesn't necessarily mean we know much more about it.* Another problem, of course, is always going to be that one of the key symptoms of a number of mental health conditions is not wanting to talk to anyone. And that can lead to lonely places.

One afternoon, at the age of fifteen, I drank half a bottle of vodka along with forty unfamiliar pills from the cupboard under the sink. I lay down on the squeaky leather sofa and got ready to disappear. My mum came home unexpectedly. Blearily, I confessed to having done something stupid and an ambulance was called.

It turned out the pills were some kind of cholesterol medication. The doctors could find no known case of overdose by them and weren't sure what to do. We waited. My leg spasmed

---

* It seems to mean, mostly, that people are now happier to label themselves as having certain disorders, while doing nothing to address the fundamental problems that lead to such disorders in the first place.

a bit, a hangover started to creep in, but otherwise I was safe. I was made to attend two counselling sessions with a well-meaning therapist before being released back into the wild. My parents were furious. I felt humiliated. Nothing changed; in fact things got worse.

Mental health was a world that I swam forward into alone. I was convinced I knew how things worked. I was convinced I knew how I worked. I let my own misguided ideas about depression, anxiety, and faulty brains shape my life for the worse. More suicide attempts followed, along with years of self-medication and never getting in the least bit better.

I'm telling you all this to show you just how easy it is for a kid to get mental health wrong. It is not about finding the right diagnosis but about finding the right cure: the cure for disconnection, for alienation, for loneliness. Only a fraction of young people will benefit from any kind of medication alone, though significantly more will leap at the chance to take it, because, like everyone else on the planet, they want to be happy, and pills claim to offer the simplest, fastest route to this.

When it comes to mental health, you need to not just keep up with your kids but overtake them. You need to know more than they know when they tell you they need medication. You have to be able to engage them fully because if you don't, they'll run on ahead without you, and it's a fucked-up thing to try and navigate at that age, and they'll probably get it wrong. Like I did. Like a number of my friends did. You end up looking for the wrong answers in the wrong places. Hoping for a simple fix to a problem that won't have one. You end up being isolated by a meaningless diagnosis, unable to engage in any of the things that may actually be able to alleviate your suffering.

A 2019 state of the nation survey of 7,000 British kids found having a high locus of control was one of the key protective factors in psychological health. Simply put, if kids think they have control of their lives, they're going to be happier. It follows, then, that believing you have a mental illness that is purely biochemical is going to make you less happy. I'm not saying anything about the nature of the illness itself, but about the beliefs someone may have surrounding that illness. If you think doctors with pills will be the only ones capable of fixing what is wrong with you, then you're going to be less motivated and enthusiastic about altering your routine or behaviour to try and improve things. What's the point, you might think, I'm still going to be depressed. Not only is viewing depression or anxiety as a spontaneous brain malfunction often seemingly incorrect in such cases, it's an idea that could prevent recovery in itself.

We need to change how kids view mental illness and start finding ways to rearrange their lives in order to protect them from it. We can introduce connection, we can introduce meaning, we can work harder to implement the simple, common-sense things like sleep and structure that everyone knows can improve our mental health. Why would you seek out a pill before everything else, when we know how effective everything else can be? Medication ought to be the last resort, not the first, and it might be turned to far less frequently if we listened to each other a little better.

It isn't ever worth it to question someone's pain. But it's also not a good idea to let them become defined by it. A balance needs to be struck between acknowledging mental illness and allowing it to rule who you become. Diagnosis is always going to be a double-edged sword: it can be a relief for parents, or it can be a worry. It can mean a life sentence for young people, or it can mean a way of better understanding themselves and what they're going through.

In my case, I wish I'd never heard the phrase 'mental illness'. It's never done me any good. Any 'experts' I've come across generally work by throwing shit at your brain and waiting for something to stick. I'm glad now to be in talk therapy of a kind that doesn't linger on diagnosis but on ways of re-establishing connection with the world.

Don't forget:

- A mental health diagnosis ought to be a stepping stone on the way to health, and not an all-consuming identity. The risk with being young is that you're still searching for your own sense of self and liable to latch onto things that shouldn't define you. And as a parent you are easily led by your child.

- Medication should be a last resort for teenagers but is often the first resort for their overstretched doctors. It can have profound side effects and mean living in an altered, intoxicated state. You may not get away with telling your kids you need to go with them to the doctor to prevent groping, but you should want to know at least the basics of any outside help they're seeking.

- If a diagnosis isn't helping, look for another solution. You can know your teenager better than the *DSM* will ever be able to.

Homework:

The only way you'll ever really know which warning signs to look out for when it comes to mental health is by doing research. A lot of it. Read and watch everything you can, because even if you don't agree with it all, some of it might be life-saving. (But again, the more research you do, the more likely you are to fall into the same trap that medical students and people who read the *Daily Mail* do: seeing danger where there is none.)

Equipped with your new-found knowledge, try having a conversation about when your teenager thinks normal emotion becomes a mental health condition. At what point would they ask for help? What do they perceive is the normal amount of sadness, anxiety, or anguish a person should carry with them? Should there be any at all? Does any of it serve a purpose? It's a conversation without an answer, which doesn't make it any less vital.

Lesson Three:

They're Not All Monsters

Online relationships and their offline consequences

I

In the course of a single night on the internet, you might storm a castle with former Yugoslavians, be called a 'faggot' by an unemployed American, and wave through a webcam at dozens of Indonesian schoolgirls. It is virtually inevitable that you brush up against people from the other side of the world. It is also inevitable that some of them become friends, especially when you're young and belong to a generation in which online friendships seem no stranger than their real-life equivalents.

Around 57 per cent of fifteen-to-eighteen-year-olds report making at least one friend online.[*] For girls, this often happens through social media, and for boys it seems to occur more

_____

[*] According to a 2015 study by the Pew Research Centre.

commonly through online games. The majority of these relationships remain confined to the internet, with one American
survey suggesting that only around 20 per cent ever result in a
real-world meet-up.

In a way, it's the fact that you know they'll never involve face-to-
face interaction that means online relationships are free to become
more intense and open. There's an old idea that you can be most
honest with strangers on the train because you know they're going
to get off in a few stops and exit your life entirely. A similar rule
applies here. You know the people you're talking to will never see
you or your friends or that ditch behind the Evangelical church
where you skin up, and this gives you a degree of freedom usually
reserved for therapy sessions or MDMA-fuelled heart-to-hearts.
You can tell online friends that you dream of taking baths with
your trumpet teacher safe in the knowledge that this secret will
never get out. You can tell them you jab yourself with a compass
when you're sad. You can tell them you experimented with a
lipstick-shaped dildo one afternoon when everyone had gone to
watch the Rugby World Cup.

Throughout my teenage years, I formed a number of online
friendships, generally with girls from distant cities who liked
despondent folk music and one-shot films. Like me, these girls
tended to have some offline friends but none they felt they could
be particularly honest with. They unanimously hated their home
towns. They were invariably bored.

We would talk about music or books or how one day we'd
own vast libraries and doe-eyed whippets. More often than not,
it was these friends that helped me get through the day. Online

relationships remind you that there is a world waiting for you outside of school. They remind you that life extends further than the corner shop and that huddle of trees where condoms grow like tiny cabbages in the ground. When it feels as though you're trapped in a packed prison of idiot children, texting Jessica from Newcastle under the desk might be the one thing keeping you sane. When it feels like no one is on your side, Jake from Leeds might be the emotional backup you need.

And online interaction can also strengthen offline relationships too. For all their faults, many games are essentially immersive team-building exercises, social media keeps teens up to date with the lives of others, and messaging apps means it costs nothing to continue conversations outside of school hours. The internet also means they will have similar touchpoints come Monday morning. Did you see the monobrowed woman doing the goose sounds? Did you watch the new BTS video? Did you hear about that woman who was assassinated for inadvertently joking about amputees?

In a sense, this levels the playing field slightly. Many experiences are now available for free to everyone, not just to the kids with money and freedom. It is no longer even the case that you have to own certain games to be able to talk about them. Every under-thirteen I know has devoted at least some time to watching videos of other people playing games they're too young and poor to own. They watch with glee as armed men roam San Andreas, or as Arthur Morgan and his band of outlaws struggle against government forces while attempting to take control of the Wild West. I don't know whether this says something about how good games have become or how little younger kids have started to expect from entertainment,* but it does at least mean no one is left out.

II

Inevitably, these online connections can develop into something else. Teenagers end up discovering both masturbation partners and long-term loves while staring into a screen.

Unsurprisingly, LGBTQ people report being more likely to start romantic relationships online than straight teenagers, probably because of the difficulty inherent in finding a partner who'll admit to not being straight in a smaller town. In this respect, the internet can give LGBTQ young people the chance to form meaningful romantic relationships at the same time as many of their peers, where previously they may have had to wait until they moved away to larger cities.

Talking to Erica, Kate,† and old schoolfriends who'd had a number of partners when we were younger, it became very clear that whether or not a relationship begins on the internet, it is likely to be shaped by it. First loves are always intense, but online communication allows that intensity to reach new levels at a breakneck pace. You never have to be physically apart from the person you are infatuated with. Digitally at least, you can be

---

* I once watched my cousin play *Heavy Rain* right the way through. This took ten hours.

† Age thirteen and fourteen, from Derby and New Zealand respectively.

by their side every second of the day. Unlimited freedom to message a person means that two individuals can become incredibly close incredibly quickly. Every moment of the day can be shared and picked over, every feeling discussed and dissected. Where once a series of staggered dates may have led to a series of more regular rendezvous, relationships can leap from an initial meeting or message to round-the-clock emotional repartee in the space of a few days.

Imagine: a love-struck Oscar messages Imogen as soon as he wakes up.

Oscar: Good morning, babe. Are you awake?

Imogen: Yes, babe, just got up.

Oscar: What are you having for breakfast, babe?

Imogen: What are *you* having for breakfast, babe?

Oscar: I asked you first, babe.

Imogen: Probably just some cheddar.

Oscar: I thought you weren't going to have cheese for breakfast any more, babe?

Imogen: I know, babe, but I'm tired and I really don't want to go to school.

Oscar: I don't want to go to school either, babe.

Imogen: Babe, I wish we could just not go to school together forever.

Oscar: Babe, that would be the best.

As he gets dressed, Oscar listens to the new Phoebe Bridgers song Imogen has sent over. He texts her a picture of a flattened hedgehog on his way to school. When he gets there, he sends her a *Rick and Morty* gif. He messages her under his desk during English. He messages her in the toilet. He messages her while he's midway through a crust-less ham sandwich in the canteen.

After school, they meet for half an hour on the bank of a stream strewn with Coke cans and taste-test each other's oral cavities. Skipping home, Oscar messages Imogen. Eating dinner, Oscar messages Imogen. Pulling the duvet over his head, Oscar messages Imogen. As dawn breaks, the cycle begins again.

No one I spoke to claimed that their interactions were desperately important. Though there may have been moments of sincerity and insight, mostly they acknowledged that they were often doing little more than procrastinating. Why struggle over supplementary angles when you can debate the relative merits of Billie Eilish's sartorial choices? I know the majority of my interactions were concerned with absolutely nothing. We talked to each other because we could, because we had free texts and Instant Messenger; we did not talk to each other because we had anything to say.

All of this means that when a relationship ends, it's all the more painful. For Oscar, he is not just losing a person he awkwardly fumbled with in the shadows, he is losing the person he spoke to every spare moment of every day. He suddenly finds himself in possession of vast swathes of empty time. He stares forlornly at a consolatory beans on toast, wishing he had someone to describe it to.

When we're in love, we want to know as much as we can about the other person: how they feel about K-pop, whether they've tried foie gras, if they think communism is a truly viable system. The internet is perfect for this. But wanting to know more and more about a person can morph quite easily into more sinister, controlling behaviour. There will always be scraps of information, photos or rumours that can prod a (probably male) partner into fits of jealousy, once he realizes that his girlfriend has a life that extends beyond him. A conversation that plays out again and again goes something like:

Girlfriend: Who's that girl who liked your last photo on Insta?

Boyfriend: Which girl?

Girlfriend: You know which girl.

Boyfriend: I don't even know which picture.

Girlfriend: The one where you're pretending to fart on Dan's face.

Boyfriend: I wasn't pretending.

Girlfriend: So you do know which picture! Who is that girl?

Boyfriend: Which girl?

Girlfriend: So there's more than one girl?

Boyfriend: I don't know what you're on about.

Girlfriend: What I'm on about is Cameltoe45.

Boyfriend: That's Liza Berry.

Girlfriend: Who the fuck is Liza Berry?

Boyfriend: Who the fuck is Steve Shipton?

Girlfriend: Steve who?

Boyfriend: Steve who posted on your wall that he's looking forward to the weekend.

Girlfriend: Steve's my cousin, you stupid prick.

Boyfriend: Since when did you have a cousin called Steve?

Girlfriend: Since fifteen years ago when my aunt shat him out.

Boyfriend: You never spoke about your cousin before.

Girlfriend: When do we speak about our cousins?

Boyfriend: Show me your messages.

Girlfriend: What?

Boyfriend: Prove that you're not messaging other guys.

Girlfriend: You're being ridiculous.

Boyfriend: If I'm being ridiculous, why wouldn't you show me?

It's not a new kind of argument, but I'd guess it's far more common since the advent of social media. One study claimed that more than half of teenagers had been in a relationship in which their partner attempted to monitor or control their behaviour.* I know a number of girls, both friends and family, who have been forced by angry boyfriends to surrender their social media log-in details, offer up sent texts, and delete photos deemed 'too revealing'. This is connected to the wild insecurity that a life lived online can provoke. Am I good enough? How do I compare to these other people? I can see there are a thousand people better than me, and what if one of them messages her? She'll almost definitely leave me for him, especially if he's not such a dick about what she does on the internet.

---

* Study conducted by Avon as part of their 2017 'Define the Line' initiative.

The internet ought to be a place of freedom, yet in many relationships it becomes another tool of abuse and control. It's such
a recent phenomenon that many young women go into it unsure
of how they should respond. Maybe he should be allowed to
read my messages? Maybe he has a right to tell me I can't accept
friend requests from men? Maybe this is normal? Maybe this is
how I prove my love?

It's a sad, distressing state of mind. Clearly a relationship isn't
healthy or heading anywhere happy when rules like that are being
scratched into its foundations. I think it would be helpful for parents to tell their children that their emails, their accounts, and their
messages ought to belong only to them.* They shouldn't have to
prove anything to a partner. No matter how close twenty-four-hour
communication might make them feel, they should never have to
surrender their intimate messages, especially not for a relationship
that is statistically likely to have ended before they've decided which
GCSEs to take (although imparting this kernel of wisdom is never
going to make you any friends amongst your offspring).

Acting without a sense of perspective is one of the most dangerous, frustrating parts of being a teenager. It is why Louise will
forego all exam revision to slink around town kicking rocks into
pigeons with Matt. It is why Dan will hang himself after hearing
that news of his wet dream has spread through school. It is why
John and Ali will think that their relationship is the single most
important feature of their lives, to be protected, nurtured, and
maintained at any cost.

---

* And to GCHQ, should they contain the words fertilizer, detonator, or plot.

It isn't always easy to know when the line is crossed from insecurity or concern to manipulation and abuse. It is worth making sure teenagers know there is a line so that they might think twice before they're backed up over it. We often talk about teaching kids boundaries – don't let strange men in the supermarket hug you, don't get into vans, don't arrange to meet faceless online avatars in shadowy alleys – but these boundaries have yet to be so clearly defined when it comes to internet etiquette while in a relationship. If you don't discuss these boundaries with your kids, they may not even realize that they ought to exist. Teens should know they have a right to privacy, online as much as in the real world, and that this right doesn't disappear the moment they enter into a partnership. It can be a stretch to ask adolescents in love to act like sane human beings but checking that their insecurities aren't snowballing into acts of cruelty or thoughtlessness can make a world of difference.

III

One of the biggest impacts of the internet on modern relationships is that it prevents you from ever really having to say goodbye. Few people enter your life and then leave without a trace. Even once sacredly temporary holiday friendships are protracted by social media into lifelong back-and-forths. You might share a kidney-shaped pool in Majorca with Norman for a week then spend the rest of your life seeing pictures whenever he adopts a new pet, eats a four seasons pizza, or drunkenly falls asleep on the grass verge beside his house.

This also means you have ever-increasing circles of friends and an ever-smaller amount of time to spend talking to each of them. Responding becomes a chore, especially when the other party can see that you've read their message and not replied.

The consequence of keeping so many 'friends' so visibly in your life is that you inevitably end up comparing your life to the lives of those around you. Keeping up with the Joneses is no longer only a game played by middle-aged suburbanites – it is the national sport. We don't only compare cars, we compare six-packs, brunches, yoga poses, and even emotional states. Is the beach they're on whiter than the one we visited? Are her boyfriend's eyes more turquoise than my boyfriend's? Is she happier than I am? Healthier? Closer to spiritual enlightenment?

Growing up in this kind of race is emotionally destabilizing. At a time when losing perspective is perilously easy, it encourages you to see things not for what they are, but for what they could appear to be to others. You end up barrelling around a desert island beach trying to draw a giant picture, invisible to you, but impressive to passing helicopters. You become obsessed with what these passing helicopter pilots think of you. Your emotional well-being becomes dependent on having these passing pilots give you a thumbs up through the cockpit window. Of course this is important, why would you doubt that? It's all you've ever seen.

It's not only friendships, but romantic relationships too that become emotionally drawn out thanks to the internet. If, God forbid, Imogen ever forsakes Oscar for a boy she considers more mature because he owns a Volkswagen Polo, then Oscar is going to be in trouble. He'll be depressed, that's a given. He'll be weepy.

He'll be heartbroken. But rather than weep fondly over old photos of the two of them together, he's more likely to look on furiously at new photos of Imogen and Raphael, fingers intertwined as the sun behind them sets in iPhone-altered shades of pink.

When a teenage relationship ends, as they tend to do, it is usually because one partner pulls the lever of the trapdoor that the other is standing on. It is not a decades-long marriage that has paled into friendship, it is an unexpected and devastating end to an intense few weeks. One party is left grieving while the object of their grief swans around on Instagram, seeming to all the world to be happier than she's ever been. You know how acutely you felt the pain of loss and missing out as a teenager; now imagine that you receive constant updates on the person you've lost and the fun they're having without you.

On another level, social media can form a swirling undercurrent to family dynamics, especially for divorced parents. Once upon a time, it would have been the case that if you chose to separate from David (because he'd become unrecognizable compared to the man you married), then he would be out of the children's lives, other than for prearranged McDonald's trips and the occasional football match. Social media has changed this entirely. Dad will not be gone from the children's lives once he is gone from the house. The parenting will not now be left entirely to you. He is probably on Facebook. He is probably on Instagram. He has access, round the clock, to the children. Not only does he have the benefit of being the fun, ice-cream offering, twenty-pound-note toting, responsibility-free parent, but he can continue to implant ideas and contest decisions.

He can hover endlessly over the lives of the children, virtu-ally sending money and leaving chirpy comments under new photographs.

You cannot banish people from your children's lives.

'You're not to see that boy any more!' intoned the parents of old.

Such pleas are becoming pointless in an age when everyone from your reception class to the barista in Costa are only few thumb flicks away. No one is ever gone, no one is ever out of reach. You cannot keep your children from interacting with anyone, be it their unsuitable ex or yours, all you can do is engineer a rela-tionship in which they feel comfortable telling you who they're spending digital time with.

IV

When I was thirteen, I spent a lot of time hiding behind an online alter ego. He shared my name but was twenty-four. He worked 'in the financial sector'. He was shy but not sexually inexperienced. He enjoyed puns, romantic fantasies, and the music of Conor Oberst. He had a malfunctioning webcam. He talked in a growl.

Catfishing is the name given to the act of pretending to be someone else on the internet. My alter ego spoke to whoever would speak to him. For the most part, this consisted of middle-aged women on the other side of the Atlantic. One woman in particular became a frequent chat partner. I'll call her Monica, because she vaguely looked like the world's most famous Monica, from the apparently immortal nineties sitcom and current most-watched

show on Netflix, *Friends*. Monica didn't know she was speaking
to a teenager. I don't know if this is because she genuinely didn't
suspect anything, didn't care if I was lying, or didn't want to enter-
tain the possibility of having wasted so long talking to an imposter.
Regardless of what she thought, we spoke regularly for close to
a year. For me, these were experimental months of self-harming,
insomnia, and initial forays into drink and drugs. For Monica,
they were some of the first months of splitting the kids with her
ex-husband.

The term catfishing came into being after a 2010 documentary
of the same name in which two brothers from New York City
begin corresponding with the mother of an eight-year-old art
prodigy in rural Michigan. Through friends of friends, they begin
interacting with various members of the girl's family through
Facebook and one of the brothers starts up a relationship with
her older sister. It becomes romantic. The sister sends videos of
herself singing, which enchant the brother until he discovers that
they're stolen from elsewhere on the internet. The brother prods
for answers but gets none.

The denouement of the documentary comes when the two
brothers travel to rural Michigan to get to the bottom of the
mystery. They are shocked by what they discover: there is no
eight-year-old art prodigy, no older sister, and none of the other
siblings they'd been made aware of. The only existent member
of the clan is the mum, who in fact lives with her husband and
his two severely disabled children from a previous marriage. She
had created fake social media accounts for each of her imagined
children and had been running them in an elaborate web, leaving

comments on each other's pages, as well as maintaining accounts of non-existent friends and more distant family members.

I could understand her behaviour entirely. She was trapped, and the internet offered an escape. She didn't have the life she'd dreamed of, so she invented it. It was escapism, like Harry Potter, LARPing*, and daydreaming about the existence of a world in which your husband is replaced by Jason Momoa.

For me, as a teenager, the appeal lay in living out fantasies of maturity and adulthood, as well as being able to try different identities on for size before having to settle on my own. It offered a connection to the adult world that I so desperately longed for. Finally, here was someone who talked to me as though I was the person I felt myself to be, rather than a mere dependant to be clothed and fed and shuttled to and from school.

Sometimes this strayed into territory that, even to me, felt jarring. One morning, by my own admittedly clumsy calculations, it must have been before school in England so around 4 a.m. in Ottawa. Monica was drinking wine. Monica often talked about drinking wine. I only drank vodka and cider, and only on weekends with friends in parks (I'd yet to fall into the arms of drinking alone).

Me: You okay?
Monica: Not really.
Me: Oh.
Monica: Things are hard.

---

* Live action roleplaying, in which people dress up as MMORPG characters and prowl around forests jabbing each other with foam swords.

This was not our agreement. Usually she would tell me she was touching herself and I told her I was touching myself and then we imagined holidays in the Alps and whole days spent lounging in bed. Sometimes she insisted on voice or video chats. During voice chats, I purposely pitched my voice down until I sounded like an identity-concealed witness in a crime documentary. During video chats, I unscrewed all but one of the little halogen bulbs in my bedroom light and put on something from my stepdad's wardrobe.

Me: What's wrong?

Monica: Just the kids' dad is being a bastard.

Me: Oh.

Monica: And I'm stuck here out in the middle of nowhere, doing nothing all day. It's just tough, you know? When the kids aren't here, I barely bother getting out of bed. I lie around thinking, what's the point? When they're not here, it's like, why the fuck am I here? What the fuck am I supposed to do? And nobody gives a shit.

It is not very often as a teenager that you have an adult speak to you candidly about their personal problems, especially concerning their children. It gives you one of those startling glimpses into the future: a suggestion that adulthood might not be the romantic, hedonistic, unending party of freedom you've been preparing for. It might just be this, but a little worse: the same fears and feelings, the same doubts and desires, only with no one around to wash your clothes or make your dinner or guide you gently back to bed when you find yourself wandering blearily around a hotel complex in the early hours of the morning.

Me: I have to go. I have to do my files.
Monica: I'm sorry.
Me: My important tax document files.
Monica: I'm sorry for talking about this.
Me: Goodbye.

I now realize I may not, as I prefer to remember, have been a positive ray of light in that woman's life.

Catfishing was once the number-one worry for parents of internet-using kids. For many, it still is. When I brought up the possibility of online friends with one mum of two young teen-agers, she started shaking her head so vigorously I could hear the bones in her neck creaking.

'No,' she said. 'I just don't agree with that. They won't be doing that.'

Which seems to me like not agreeing with electric scooters or Brexit: they are happening anyway. In truth, parents would be better off worrying about themselves. In the past two months, I've heard of the mums of two friends getting scammed out of significant sums of money online, whereas this set of kids are so well versed in the internet that they're unlikely to fall for a Hebridean llama farmer claiming he's the proud owner of pendulous breasts. They know the methods used to deceive. They probably invented them.

Anyone claiming to be a woman while posting on the popular

anarchic forum 4chan is heavily scrutinized. Before the idea that she is female will even be taken seriously, she must first post a picture of herself holding a sign with the date, time, and name of the board handwritten on it. This picture will then be closely investigated for signs of doctoring. Shadows will be analysed, pixels will be blown up and squinted over. Once it has been certified as genuine, then, and only then, will the 4chan dwellers be at all interested in seeing badly shot photos of their female guest's anatomy, or asking her questions about how best to approach a woman without having her make the sound she usually reserves for discovering a wad of hair in the plughole.

Joel Dommett is a thirty-three-year-old British comedian who appeared on the 2017 incarnation of *I'm a Celebrity. . . Get Me Out of Here*. A month later, a video of him happily masturbating at a webcam surfaced. Some time before being airdropped into the Australian jungle, he was messaged by an account pretending to be an attractive young woman. She asked him to Skype and he agreed. During that Skype session, he masturbated. He thought he was watching her do the same, when in fact he was watching a pre-recorded video taken from a pay-to-watch cam site.

As we've seen, it's dangerous on the internet for the digitally naive. Generally, this means older people. I don't know anyone who would be stupid enough to happily masturbate on camera with their face in full view, especially not someone who's come of age knowing that every aspect of their existence will be catalogued online for years to come. It happens, of course, and when it does there can be disastrous consequences, but a lot of kids know instinctively not to leave yourself vulnerable. Naked selfies are generally taken without distinguishing features, such as tattoos or unusual piercings (more on this in chapter 7), photos are traded not given, and transient forms of communication like webcams and Snapchat are preferred for online sex.

The relationship with Monica petered out when real girlfriends became more serious. Still, some of my first sexual experiences involved listening to a woman who looked very slightly like Courtney Cox going to town on herself with a black dildo on the other side of the Atlantic Ocean. There is something both soul-shattering and exhilarating about the first time you realize that adults are idiots too, just as clueless and forlorn.

Generally, I look back on those long nights spent at the keyboard with great fondness. They made me the rapid and accurate typist that I am today. I wish Monica all the best.

V

It can be easier to maintain online relationships than flesh-and-blood ones. You are less likely to fall out with Polly from the Netherlands because she isn't hovering over you all the time, breathing breakfast breath and begging you for your last Mini Cheddar. She is only there when you need to talk, ready to trade pornographic fantasies, intimate confessions, and bathroom selfies.

It can mean that emotional support is more readily available, that friendships can be built even amongst those who find the prospect of face-to-face interaction terrifying, and that we have the chance to know each other better than ever before. It also means we are free to embark on secret lives from the comfort of our beds, adding new depths to our personae and make ourselves less knowable than ever.

But the internet can cause mayhem for the real-world relationships of teenagers. It alters relationships by heightening the intensity of certain impulses: you can be there for someone when they need you most, you can be there for someone you've never met, you can be there for someone when they don't need you, and you can impose yourself on someone when they don't want you.

It has been said a million times by dead-eyed content creators that we are more connected but lonelier than ever. This interconnectedness means, necessarily, more manipulation, more bullying, and more arguments. We are still people. Our faults are only magnified by the distance screens put between us, our ability to treat each other badly is only made worse by the fact that we don't have to sit in front of each other and watch the emotional repercussions of our behaviour. That we are talking to each other more, but through a medium devoid of any of the physical cues that true communication hinges on, is not necessarily going to be a good thing.

If the young are speaking to each other more, expanding their relationships until they fill every available waking moment, then there is a very real possibility that they will crowd out the other pillars of a balanced life: health, work, family, and hobbies. Relationships might be a key part of emotional well-being for a young person, but they are not the only part, even if Snapchat can generate billions of dollars from peddling that very idea. Relationships alone do not lead to success or happiness or contentment; they are one dimension of a life that needs propping up at all four corners.

Part of the key here is that young people have no models for how to navigate the online element of their relationships. If they're lucky, they've grown up watching you and your partner divide up chores, listen to each other's problems, and generally do your best to look after each other, but even if this is the case, how does it translate to instant messaging and Instagram? As a child, you're told off for calling people pooheads and – when you're older, maybe – assholes, but you never learn what is and isn't okay to send someone in a text, because by the time you're old enough to send them, you're sending them privately. And where do you learn how much of someone's online activities you're allowed to have a say over? Or whether it's reasonable that your boyfriend should expect you to message him five or ten or twenty times a day?

As parents, it is up to you to let your children know that they should expect to be treated no differently on the internet than they are in real life. By being taught what they should ask of other people, teenagers can more easily distinguish between friendships and relationships that are meaningful and those that will waste their time, distract them, and lead to unnecessary pain. Nobody's first forays into romance are easy but they don't have to be as brutal as the internet has the potential to make them.

Don't forget:

- Online relationships in themselves are nothing to be afraid of. For certain teenagers, they'll be the only way of meeting like-minded people. Of course they have to be safe, but the more open you are to the possibility of online relationships, the more likely your kids will be to open up to you about them, and the safer they'll be.

- Young people need to at least think about the boundaries they should set when it comes to relationships and the digital world. You don't have to be at someone else's beck and call just because modern technology makes it possible; you shouldn't have to surrender your right to privacy to be in a relationship; and no partner should be telling you what you can and can't post, say, or engage with online.

- In the same way as you might call someone in an adjacent car names you'd never say to someone standing next to you in the supermarket, the internet can cause us to come out with surprisingly hurtful things thanks to the level of distance and separation it puts between us. Teenagers especially can need reminding that, even when it doesn't feel like it, there are real people on the other end of their satellite communications.

- It's not kind to break up with someone by Messenger. Teenagers should learn how to do it in person because facing up to the emotions of other people will prove a crucial skill in later life.

Homework:

This is a weird one, the purpose of which might not seem immediately relevant, but, if you have time, make some popcorn and watch the 2009 animated film *Mary and Max*. It's about an eight-year-old girl who strikes up a friendship with an eighty-year-old man in New York via letters. I know it's not about teenagers, or even about the internet, but it is a reminder of how unlikely friendships can be forged between people who have never met, and how these friendships can have real and powerful consequences in our lives. There is nothing inherently sinister in talking to people you don't know. It is part of being human.

Interlude 1:

Reading List for Unfinished Humans

During your teenage years, you cling to certain books, TV shows, and whole albums like lifeboats. They make you feel less lonely, offer some kind of escape, remind you of a good time, and can provide an insight into yourself and those around you. Sometimes having the right books to hand can mean the difference between outright despair and managing to get by. They are also capable of much more than just offering company; for some children, it may be that through identifying with fictional characters they can come to realizations about their own sexuality, gender, or identity.

Rather than try to cover all the bases, here is a list of books that helped me and some friends while we were going through adolescence. Of course you can't force your kids to fall in love with books, but you can leave them lying around the house or give them as presents immediately after confiscating all phones and computers. You can also get an audiobook subscription, and suggest that they might be an interesting accompaniment for journeys to school or boring car rides.

It's Kind of a Funny Story, Ned Vizzini
A novel about a boy who finds himself in a mental health ward after a suicide attempt. Ned himself committed suicide at the age of thirty-two in 2016. His books mean a lot to many kids.

The Perks of Being a Wallflower, Stephen Chbosky
The strength of this book is, I think, in its portrayal of an emotionally vulnerable and open boy, and a friendship group around him that manages to function with kindness.

Running with Scissors, Augusten Burroughs
The strangeness of the family in this memoir made me feel like mine wasn't so dysfunctional after all. Young people have a tendency to suspect that they've been born into the worst family possible, and it can be good to get a sense of perspective.

Girl, Interrupted, Susanna Kaysen
The memoir of an eighteen-year-old girl in a psychiatric ward after a suicide attempt. The film, starring Winona Ryder and Angelina Jolie, managed to turn a quite painful account of hopelessness into something altogether more unpalatable.

Mind Your Head; *This Book is Gay*; *The Gender Games*, Juno Dawson
I wish these had been out a few years earlier so I could have had them when I needed them. Dawson writes so lucidly and

engagingly about sex, gender, mental health, and growing up, that it's hard to imagine better introductions to them for teens.

A Season in Hell, Arthur Rimbaud

Because it can help to have very pretty elucidations of your despair written by other teenagers who have felt similarly despairing.

Love That Dog, Sharon Creech

Written entirely as a series of free-verse poems, this is the story of a boy forced to write poetry in class and slowly, reluctantly, learning how to use it as a means of expression. It was the first time I learned about what poetry could really do.

Call Me by Your Name, André Aciman

I mean, for obvious reasons.

The Outsiders, S.E. Hinton

Possibly the most famous novel in the American canon of young adult literature. It's not bad, you know. And it does a good job of warning against the perils of peer pressure and trying to fit in.

Oranges Are Not the Only Fruit, Jeanette Winterson

A wonderful book about discovering your sexuality, and about the claustrophobia of adolescence.

Breakfast of Champions, Kurt Vonnegut

The overriding message of Vonnegut is always that we ought to be kind and that life is incredibly strange and funny. He's helped adolescents find the humour in the pain of existence for years now. He can also help you to think of other people, even those that don't make sense to you, with a little more warmth.

When I Was Five I Killed Myself, Howard Buten

The main character is only eight in this novel, but something about his rage to be understood in a world that seems bent on not hearing him meant it became one of my favourite books from the age of fourteen on. Recently, I got to write a foreword for a new edition, and I spent the time thinking about what I was going to say while hugging my battered old copy like a puppy.

Crush, Richard Siken

The poetry of Richard Siken is a long-time teenage favourite on the internet. It's beautiful, it's sad, it's strange, and it's romantic in an unobvious way.

Lesson Four:

A Field Guide to the Hinterlands of the Internet

School shooters, the dark web, and online gambling

I

Like anywhere, the internet has its less salubrious neighbourhoods. That's not surprising. What might be surprising is how readily accessible and popular some of these spots are.

As I'm writing this, it's been three days since a twenty-eight-year-old Australian man massacred fifty people and injured fifty more in two New Zealand mosques. The shooting was live-streamed on Facebook. As he entered one of the mosques, the shooter screamed 'subscribe to PewDiePie'.*

Brenton Tarrant was heavily involved in the alt-right, a loose

---

* Aka Felix Kjellberg, a YouTuber with over 101 million subscribers and 23 billion views. Ranked number one in the 2019 *Sunday Times* influencer list.

collection of white supremacists who espouse racist, misogynist, anti-immigrant, and anti-government views through forum posts, memes, and videos. According to the anti-defamation league, the alt-right constitute the leading threat of extremist violence in America. They have been connected to a number of shootings, mostly in the US. The alt-right encompass neo-Nazism, militant atheism, Christian fundamentalism, conspiracy theories, anti-Semitism, anti-Islam, anti-LGBTQ, anti-feminism, men's rights, and various forms of anarchism and globalism.

With the election of Donald Trump, a number of key figures from the alt-right gained unprecedented levels of power and influence. Alex Jones – proponent of such ideas as 'Sandy Hook was staged' and 'the government has weather control weapons' – has been described as 'amazing' by the President of the United States. Steven Bannon – who referred to his own online news site Breitbart as 'a platform for the alt-right' – served as chief White House strategist from January 2017 until August of that year.

As is increasingly the case in the aftermath of incidents like Christchurch, police were left to follow a troubling set of footprints left across certain parts of the internet. Tarrant was a user of the imageboard site called 8chan; it was there that he posted a manifesto titled 'The Great Replacement' shortly before he committed the atrocity.

The 'manifesto' is jumbled, hate-filled, conspiracy-fuelled drivel that touches on everything from *Spyro the Dragon 3* to al-Qaeda. Tarrant seemed to have held a very vague collection of nonsensical extremist ideas, which is increasingly common at a time when nonsensical extremist ideas travel far more quickly online than reasonable ones. The more outlandish an idea is, the more likely it is to be shared on the internet. In the same way that three minutes of Crazy Frog making car sounds was once number one in eight countries, bizarre conceptions can spread between internet users purely because they are bizarre. No one, after all, is going to share a story saying that the moon landings happened, 9/11 was committed by the Taliban, or Brittany Murphy was not killed by reptilian members of the Illuminati.

It might seem unlikely that your teenager would gravitate towards this kind of content. But often the content gravitates towards you, rather than the other way around.

Let's go back to YouTube for a second. As we saw in chapter 1, YouTube does not give a shit about whether you have an enjoyable or fulfilling time on YouTube: it just wants you to stay on YouTube for as long as possible, and then come back as soon as possible and do the same thing all over again. One of the key tactics it uses to do this is providing a list to the right of whatever you're currently watching of other videos you might like to watch next. Most teenagers I spoke to said that what they watch on YouTube is generally 'whatever comes up in the suggestions bar really'. This is where problems can arise.

For all its rules against showing nipples and avoiding copyright infringement, YouTube is more than happy to point you down rabbit holes of increasingly extreme and unsettling content. It knows that by always making these suggestions slightly more shocking or strange than whatever you're currently watching, it'll keep you on the site.

Here is a quick run-through of one of my recent YouTube spirals, during which I was led to content you probably wouldn't be wildly enthusiastic about your kids watching:

- On my YouTube homepage, I'm immediately presented with a number of suggestions based on things I've previously watched. Currently this includes old Blink-182 concerts, James Acaster stand-up, and a video of Shaquille O'Neal being interviewed while eating a series of increasingly spicy hot wings.
- Having just read his book about free will, I decide to watch a lecture by the innocuous American philosopher Sam Harris.
- One of the suggested videos in the sidebar is of Jordan Peterson, the pseudo-intellectual self-help guru for wannabe alpha males, whose book *12 Rules for Life: An Antidote to Chaos* sold millions of copies, mostly to directionless young men.
- Now I've been taken to a video that claims to divulge FBI negotiating secrets. It features a forty-something man in a suit, speaking for forty minutes about pseudo-scientific 'psychological tricks' aimed to help you get the upper hand in negotiations. For some reason, he claims that the only country in the world apart from the USA to have birthright citizenship is Canada.
- Next up is a suggested video that features the far-right British UKIP member Tommy Robinson, explaining how

something called 'the deep state' has been persecuting him. This has 80k views, though some videos featuring him have millions.

- I am invited to listen to an audio of the 999 call made by eighteen-year-old Lewis Daynes after he murdered the fourteen-year-old Breck Bednar in 2014. Thanks, YouTube!
- Now we're back to Tommy Robinson arguing about the Quran on breakfast television.
- Next up is a video titled 'Crazy muslim cleric anjem choudary chants his shit on gmtv and ends up looking a tit'.
- Now: Muslim gang rapist has no remorse for his victims.
- The worst of Islam apologists.
- Feminist cringe compilation.
- Feminism vs Logic.

And so on, and so on, in an ever-downward spiral of backwards thinking and misdirected rage. It is not difficult to stumble onto dangerous ideas, especially if you are spending a lot of time on YouTube, and it is not a big leap from anti-Islam videos on YouTube to the frenetic anti-everything fury of chan sites and other dingy online social clubs frequented by Brenton Tarrant and other alt-right sympathizers.

Violent acts such as the terror attack in Christchurch are often traced back to the internet, committed for the internet, and completed with its help and encouragement. We still tend to associate the idea of 'radicalization' with Islam. In reality,

terrorist acts are becoming more and more likely to be committed by white men and boys radicalized on the internet.*

||

Let's dig deeper: 4chan and 8chan are the parts of the internet's
iceberg that sit largely underwater. Only after school shootings
or notable scandals do they fall under the scrutiny of mainstream
media.

One notorious example was the 2014 celebrity nude photos
leak, known as 'the fappening' on 4chan. This involved hackers
gaining access to the private accounts of a number of celebrities
through phishing scams, then posting the naked selfies they found
to the forums and private individuals, mostly in return for bitcoin,
the cryptocurrency that hit headlines in mid-2018 when the price
for a single unit of the digital currency climbed above twenty
thousand dollars. Five men were eventually arrested and given
prison sentences ranging from eight months to almost three years.

In that case, the work was done by individuals acting independently, but more frequently their real-world intrusions involve
effecting change by cooperating on a mass scale.

The sheer number of 4chan users means that if they decide
to work together, they can have a devastating impact. In 2008,
4chan users started a rumour that Steve Jobs was dead, causing

---

* The *New York Times* reported that in 2011 there were just nine white extremist
terror acts committed in North America, Europe, and Australia combined. In 2015
this figure was 135.

Apple's stock to fall by 10 per cent. In 2016, they worked out the coordinates of a group of ISIS militants from a video, sent them to a Russian army general, and prompted an airstrike. In 2013, they tricked thousands of young people into self-harming in support of Justin Bieber by launching the hashtag #cuttingfor-bieber, supposedly as an attempt to get him to stop smoking. In 2012, when a campaign was announced to name a new flavour of Mountain Dew, 4chan users rigged the vote so that the top result came out as 'Hitler did nothing wrong'.

Sites like 4chan are organized by theme. These range from science and maths to hardcore porn and anime. Each of them has a board on which anyone is free to post anything they want, the only rule being that the initial post is accompanied by a picture. The pace is frenetic. Posts that receive frequent replies (called 'bumps') stay near the top of the board. Posts that fall off the edge of the thirtieth page are deleted forever. All posts are completely anonymous. Although there are moderators, their only real role is to delete posts containing child porn and to make sure people aren't posting in the wrong places.

The most notorious board on 4chan is /b/, the board for 'random' posts. This is where the majority of the most notorious pranks and hoaxes have sprung from.

I've just now opened the /b/ board on 4chan, and the first thread starts with a photograph of three underage girls* and people answering the question 'which one would you fuck?';

---

* You might ask 'Where are those moderators?!' As long as the children in the pictures are wearing clothes, there doesn't seem to be a problem with people fantasizing about sex with them.

the second thread is people sharing links to downloads of the Christchurch massacre video; the third poses the question: 'She cheats on you, b, what do you do?' Some of the answers read:

Cocaine with this slut I knew from before I met my gf. I was planning on fucking her too but I had coke dick.* Kind of a shitty night tbh.

Punched her, physically threw her out of my apartment, drank an 8 pack.
Good times. Been single since. Staunchly anti hookup culture. 4 years of no sex.

Hid in the closet and jerked off as she was cucked by this Muslim black guy. Once I had blown my load I tried to sneak away but they caught me and called me names like 'little man' as I hobbled away, hunched over with cold Jizz still dripping from my flaccid sticky cock.
Fuck I am diamonds† just thinking about it.

The next time a Muslim prepares to go about slaughtering our innocents he will re-think his position knowing that a westerner might ascend to the level of Templar Knight and waste his local mosque, killing every last family member 'innocent' he loves.

---

* An inability to achieve an erection due to the vasoconstricting properties of cocaine.
† Diamonds means your penis is extremely hard.

Brenton Tarrant was a fucking hero.

Reported her and her family to ICE*.

She cheated on me with a guacamole. Needless to say, she's back in shitholiostan, Mexico. Friend of mines says she's preggers now.

Pic related [link to a gallery of pictures on a popular porn site, titled 'american whore']

Put her on the internet.

Got her little brother hooked on heroin and had her mom admitted into a mental hospital by convincing her that she was responsible for her son's problems and addiction.

Too much time spent on 4chan will hijack your internal monologue. Regardless of whether you agree with anything being said, the voice will lodge itself in your head, especially if you're young, and your own voice hasn't cemented itself yet.

This is the more anarchic, public side of that brand of vitriol, but there are more private areas of the internet where men's rights activists, white nationalists and incels (involuntary celibates who are part of the alt-right online subculture) flourish. There, the ideas that are kicked around in threads like the one above are picked over and outlined in greater detail. They tend to revolve

---

* Immigration and Customs Enforcement in the US. Formed after 9/11 and now the frequent target of rage thanks to their inhumane raids on undocumented immigrants.

around blaming women and minorities for their misery and misfortune, as well as plotting ways to seek revenge.

Men's rights proponents talk about taking the 'red pill', or realizing that traditional gender roles were created to benefit women rather than men. In contrast, incels talk about taking the 'black pill', or understanding that, for certain men, there is no chance of ever being with women, purely because they were born 'unattractive' and there is nothing beyond looks, power, or wealth involved in sex.

It is that angry, warped, self-entitled ideology that makes incels so dangerous. Four mass shootings have been linked to online incel communities. Along with boards like 4chan, incels tend to mythologize and look up to infamous mass murderers like Dylann Roof, the young white supremacist who killed nine African Americans in a church in North Carolina, and Anders Breivik, the far-right Norwegian terrorist who killed seventy-seven people in Utøya and Oslo, supposedly to save Europe from an influx of Muslims.

What the online antics of 4chan users and real-life violence of men like Tarrant do is offer the feeling of power to the powerless. Swept up in exaggerated language and unrealistic fantasies, people can begin to believe that their deranged imaginings hold some truth. If you are emotionally isolated enough and interacting only with people who talk like those in the 4chan thread above, you'd be hard pressed to escape getting swept up in it. It might be a darker echo chamber than many of the cotton-lined neoliberal ones, but they all work the same way: you have a set of followers or readers, you post something knowing they'll agree with it, then you revel in their likes and positive feedback. You prefer the positive feedback to the negative. It makes you feel better. So you shrink your online world until it consists of a large circle of people nodding furiously at each other. You shrink your world until everyone thinks like you.

With sites like 4chan, this causes another problem: the ever-present element of role play makes it impossible to tell who is being genuine and who is being reactionary. How do you know which posts to take seriously when every single one is threatening rape or murder? This is a difficult issue for trained investigators, let alone for teenagers with no help or guidance. If they believe that all of the anonymous posters really are doing the cruel and violent things they claim, then it is all the more easy to get swept up in the hatred. While everyone else might be playing a game, a handful of vulnerable teenagers might not be in on the joke.

III

Parents, why am I telling you all this?

Because you need to know about this stuff. No other parenting book will be teaching you these things. The cliché that those of a certain age don't understand computers is quite appropriate when it comes to parenting. Studies show that the older you are, the more likely you are to share 'fake news'. It's fair enough, I guess, that the internet came into the lives of today's baby boomers a little too late for them to ever fully comprehend it. But even now, twenty years on, ridiculous hoaxes spread like wildfire amongst them. As I'm writing, thousands of grown adults have fearfully shared stories of a birdlike character called Momo telling children to commit atrocious acts of violence through iPads. Not true. Also as I'm writing, one relative received a note from her child's school warning parents that fake, hallucination-inducing treats called 'astrosnacks' were being sold to children outside the play-ground. Not only untrue, but unbelievable, because who would want to waste valuable hallucinogenic drugs? And still, every year, at Halloween, the internet manages to convince parents that strangers are going to be putting needles, razors, and LSD into the sweets they hand out to children. This has never once happened.

I remember the first time I witnessed an adult's misplaced trust in the internet.

A few days after 9/11, my mum got a breathless call from my uncle.

'Turn on the computer right now,' he told her.

'What? Why?'

'Just do it, and call me back as soon as you've done it.'

She pulled open the door of the cupboard under the stairs and booted up our big, yellowing Windows 98-running desktop computer.

'Now open Microsoft Word,' said my uncle.

'Okay.'

'The number of one of the flights to hit the towers was Q33NY. Type that in, change it to size 48.'

'I've done it.'

'Now change the font to Wingdings.'

She did it.

'Oh my God,' she shouted, aghast. 'No!'

The screen was showing:

✈ 📄 📄 ☠ ✿

For my mother, this would mark the beginning of a number of years spent forwarding chain emails and only narrowly avoiding confidence scams. It also meant a conviction that computers were full of evil, a conviction that manifested itself in frequent, covert trawls through my internet history.

As a parent, you may well think you are outwitting your off-spring when it comes to computers.

You might well think that modern controls mean there's no way kids can roam the cyber world freely. Well, you are wrong. When I told one mother I was working on this book, she said I should explain to parents how to monitor what their teenagers have been doing on the internet.

'You should tell them to check their browser history,' she said. 'Then they can tell what their children have been looking at.'

If your child is younger than eleven this might work out, but if they've grown even a single pubic hair, I doubt it's going to bear much fruit. I was surprised that anyone still had faith in parental security controls on computers. I learned very early on that looking at porn meant either going through a proxy or deleting the history afterwards. I learned this, in fact, before my parents did. I knew what they looked at and they knew what I wanted them to think I looked at. Sometimes I would purposely google things like 'how many turnips are there in the world?' hoping that they wouldn't be able to resist bringing these up in conversation. They never did.

Parents, know that you can password-protect your browser settings so the history can't be deleted, but kids can always get to boobs and beheadings through proxies, VPNs, and a thousand other not-particularly-dark alleyways. It doesn't really matter what these are, only that they are unstoppable. The only way to really monitor what a young person is doing on the internet is to stand right behind them, or install keyboard logging software on their computer. This will track every keystroke made by the user of a computer within whatever time frame you ask it to. It will, especially if they've been doing homework, take a very long time to look through. It might also make your child hate you.

I don't think my mum being able to see my genuine internet history would have helped either of us much. In fact, it would have probably led her to think I was a far worse person that I (hope I) am.

I am not a psychopath. I cry during Pixar films and become inconsolable if I think I've even mildly upset anyone. But, like many young people, from the ages of fourteen to eighteen, I watched: a kitten being stamped to death by a woman in heels; suicides by hanging, electrification, stabbing, and shooting; mangled bodies spread across pavements; beheadings, hangings, amputations, the aftermath of gruesome accidents, and videos of women having sex with dogs and horses.

Aside from feeling uncomfortable about the ethical issues of killing and having sex with animals, I don't think that seeing any of these did any lasting damage or signalled any severe empathy deficit. I watched them purely because they were there. People slow down while passing accidents. With the internet you can witness every accident that's ever happened, slowed down, and zoomed in so far you can watch an eyeball slowly rolling along the asphalt.

Snuff videos function in the same way that horror films do: for the most part, you watch them to be scared, frightened, and shocked. You watch them to feel jolted out of your normal state, to have your heart jump-started and your sense of normality disrupted. Most people who watch them are not serial killers or psychopaths. I'm sure a number of serial killers have watched videos like these, but I'm sure they also have every *Saw* film on Blu-ray. If you want gore, modern films are far more repulsive than real videos of blood and guts. And I doubt the physical or emotional response to seeing acts like that on a screen is vastly different to seeing something that's labelled as the real thing.

That's not to say that I don't think the internet isn't a playground for the morally dubious, but weirdos have been killing cats for a long time; they haven't needed the internet to give them the idea.*

You cannot protect your child from seeing and hearing terrible things; you can only protect them from getting lost amongst them. Oscar is going to have to wander into the dark forest of dangerous things at some point. You can either deny that this will happen or you can send him in prepared, armed with knowledge of the creatures that lie in wait. And it sounds obvious, but it isn't. As I mentioned previously, most parents will refuse even to

* By the way, if you ever catch your child unrepentantly killing animals, the only possible reasonable outcome I can imagine is that of the TV show *Derek*: you train your psychopathic son to satisfy his urges through murdering murderers.

acknowledge that their teenage sons might watch porn, let alone scroll through neo-Nazi message boards or piss money away each week on Texas hold 'em.

Although most grim facets of the internet are only visited during phases that teenagers grow out of, a bigger worry is that those in charge of legislating against it have almost no experience of how the internet actually works. It is impossible to protect young people if you do not understand the beast you are trying to keep away from them.

The British government has recently attempted to introduce mandatory age controls for porn sites. Hurrah! you cheer. Finally! No more free pounding for the under-nines!

In theory, wonderful. In practice, more like locking the door but leaving the window wide open. It's a huge waste of time, effort, and money. With a few clicks, they can add a VPN extension to their Chrome browser that will let them circumvent the expensive 'Do Not Enter' sign the government is proposing. Children who want to play blocked games on school computers know this, but apparently government ministers don't. Another part of their plan would have over-eighteens physically go and buy porn passports from shops – an idea as stupid as selling hallucinatory astrosnacks to schoolchildren.

IV

You should probably be more afraid of your kids gambling than looking at porn or ISIS executions.

A 2018 UK study suggested that more eleven-to-sixteen-year-olds gamble regularly than smoke, drink, or take drugs. Gambling has become easier than ever, which really means that it has become easier than ever for bookmakers to take your money. With a few taps of an app, you can lose half the month's rent on two spins of a slot and the other half on a horse called Dream World. If you let gambling get its hooks in early, it will be a demon that sits on your kid's shoulder for life. The feeling that a single win can inspire is more than enough to make them forget a hundred thousand losses.

Fixed-odds betting terminals have been the form of gambling to receive some of the most coverage in recent years. These are the digital machines that sit in bookmakers and offer a number of 'games' that look like slots. People attack the machines. People cry in front of the machines. People return to the shops in which the machines are located and assault staff with blunt instruments.

They are an unprecedentedly good way of getting money off gamblers. So good, that the government decreed that each betting shop could only have four of them. As a result, all our beloved bookmakers chose to buy up the crumbling high street charity shops and simply open more branches, sometimes immediately next to their old ones.

I have spent weeks if not months sitting in front of FOBTs and their online equivalents. Once, while playing in a bar in Berlin, I got speaking to a tired-looking man who said he'd previously owned a car dealership but lost it through the machines.

'Why do you keep going?'

He shrugged.

It's such a common story that it's almost boring.

One member of my family became trapped in cycles of payday loans and online gambling, accumulating debts that made me shiver even before he was old enough to drink in America. By the time someone had stepped in to clear his debts, he'd already accumulated more.

The modern gambling industry uses a number of insane tactics to keep people hurling money at them. Machines and online games light up, chirp, and show animations which lead you on bizarre adventures. They will ecstatically trumpet wins, even if the wins are a fraction of the cost of the turn you just took. They give you tiny rewards and make shiny promises to keep you from logging off or walking away. In the exact same way as the apps and sites designed by our Silicon Valley overlords, these games are designed to fool human brains into spitting out dopamine. They do a catastrophically good job of it. There is a reason that the rise of online gambling has occurred in tandem with the explosion in morally bankrupt payday loan companies.

All of these things make them dangerous for adults, and even more dangerous for almost-adults, whose brain elasticity makes them ripe for becoming addicted to anything the world wants to shove their way. But although traditional gambling is worryingly common amongst teenagers, many get their first taste via gaming in other forms, such as 'loot boxes'. These are boxes earned or found in games that can be 'opened' to reveal items of varying worth. Some items are rare and valuable, most are not. These boxes can also be bought for actual money, and their contents traded or sold, essentially making them nothing more than dressed-up gambling.

Physical 'mystery boxes' are another method of gambling popular amongst the under-twenties. These are boxes generally containing an assortment of designer shoes or clothes, bought, you hope, for less than the total value of the items, so that a profit can be made from selling them on. Videos purporting to show YouTubers opening mystery boxes have millions of views. The majority of the time, these YouTubers receive wonderful things. I am ashamed to admit that I have spent hours wiling away time watching nauseatingly upbeat YouTubers* gleefully lift Kanye West-designed shoes out of boxes covered in cartoon question marks. When their viewers purchase the same boxes, I doubt they have the same experiences. They furtively save up for boxes of cheap, disappointing tat, while the YouTubers in cahoots with mystery box companies sun themselves on yachts equipped with selfie stations.

Studies have shown that even mock, moneyless forms of gambling embedded in games can put children at risk of developing gambling problems later on. The dopamine hit is the same. It isn't necessarily dependent on how much money is being won or lost, but on the uncertainty of the outcome. What will come next? Your brain salivates at the prospect of finding out. And once it has learned this game, it won't forget it.

---

* Mostly I became inexplicably hooked on a young man named Harrison Nevel. For a period of two weeks, I would eat every meal in front of videos of him opening mystery boxes, cawing over their contents, and working out that the total resale value of the items within was marginally higher than what he paid for the box. I now know much more than I need to know about the kinds of shoes I will never, ever own.

One of the smartest things I ever did was put a daily limit on each of my online gambling accounts. Overnight, this turned a potentially life-ruining habit into the equivalent of secretly eating cookies in the toilet. I haven't deleted them entirely. The garish, twinkling, tinkling virtual slot machines still hold an undeniable allure and I also like putting bets on things like who the next James Bond will be (Riz Ahmed, 25/1) and which film will win best picture at the Oscars in a few weeks (*Parasite*, 9/2)*. I know I shouldn't do it, I think, but it isn't harming anyone. Still, I doubt that I'll ever shake the desire to wander into betting shops or gamble online, and I don't doubt this is because of being exposed to it at an age where I didn't have the capacity to resist.

V

After sixteen schoolchildren lost their lives in the Dunblane massacre, the UK passed laws making the private ownership of virtually all handguns illegal. There have been no school shootings here since. There have been many elsewhere, of course, some more high profile than others, and most but by no means all taking place in America. In 2009, seventeen-year-old Tim Kretschmer shot dead fifteen of his classmates in Winnenden, south-eastern Germany. In 2017, a fourteen-year-old Brazilian boy shot dead two of his classmates and injured four more. In the USA in 2018,

---

* This bet came in and I have since been around £30 richer.

there was, on average, one school shooting in every eight school-days.

When we hear of the mass murder of students in America, we count ourselves lucky for belonging to a society in which guns are not so revered.

But we can't afford to grow complacent.

The world is changing and we've come far closer to our own Columbine than we might like to imagine. I recently found evidence of this in a particularly bizarre and unexpected way.

Just over a year ago, my sister and I were having a beer with one of our younger cousins when he offhandedly mentioned that his stepbrother had recently been arrested. The stepbrother – who I'll call Sam despite his case being public – was eighteen and studying for A levels with the intention of going to university.

'What?' said my sister, perking up at the sound of gossip. 'Why?'

Because he'd ordered a gun through the dark web, paid for it in bitcoin, and had his package intercepted by Homeland Security at Newark airport, New York. They had let the local police know and the package had been swapped for one containing a dummy. Police had watched his mum sign for the delivery before raiding the house.

Upon his arrest, Sam's room was searched. Handwritten notes and a USB stick loaded with a Bible-sized research project on massacres were discovered. Although he'd been using software that wiped his browser history, police came while it was still open and could see that he'd spent the day reading about Molotov cocktails, the Columbine massacre, and how best to care for his shiny new Glock 17. It was obvious he'd been plotting some kind of mass shooting. He was obsessed with the Columbine killers as well as Anders Breivik. In court, Sam admitted to having watched execution videos from the age of thirteen. He also claimed to have looked into Molotov cocktails as a potential means of suicide, rather than through any interest in blowing up his school, an idea which sounded as stupid in court as it does written down.

'Who would ever try to commit suicide using a Molotov cock-tail?' asked the rightfully sceptical prosecution barrister.

Sam was a hapless loner, convinced that his empowerment could come through an act of violence. Perpetuating the idea that murder might be a satisfying form of revenge for someone who feels let down by society was also one of the criticisms levelled at the recent Joaquin Phoenix film, *Joker*.

In the film – this section will contain spoilers, by the way – an outcast who is belittled by colleagues, ignored by women and let down by mental health services, becomes the hero of his own story by shooting dead three men who hassle him on a train, then shooting dead the host of a TV talk show who'd earlier mocked him by airing a clip of his shitty stand-up. His act inspires people across the city to rise up against the oppressive power structures that have kept them locked in the dingy basement of an unequal society. They take to the street, faces painted in honour of the Joker, causing mayhem and destruction as they go. They even pause to free their hero from a police car and hoist him aloft. He has finally found his people. The loner is alone no more.

Many critics couldn't help but shake the feeling that the film was going to appeal to a certain demographic in ways others might not comprehend. It was, from one perspective, a film made for the Sams of the world. A film which not only empathized with them but showed them a way out of their misery. A film which showed them a means of being heard in a world which didn't seem to want to hear what they had to say.

Sam was found guilty of 'the intention to endanger life' and sentenced to sixteen years in prison. It's often said that we're too generous in our willingness to understand white perpetrators of mass shootings, especially when compared to the treatment kids of colour receive for their involvement in gang crime, but I couldn't help wondering if Sam might not have found himself in a prison cell if it wasn't for the internet. He probably would still have been diagnosed with autism and depression. He definitely wouldn't have been able to order a gun, but beyond that he wouldn't have become enmeshed in a culture that deified mass murderers and studied their atrocities. He wouldn't have found this loose society of loners, egging each other on in unspeakable thoughts and acts. He wouldn't have seen his version of *Joker*, and his rage would, you hope, likely have faded once he was free of school.

However abhorrent you may find them, however unworthy of our attempts at understanding, the only way to prevent tragedies like Columbine, Sandy Hook, and Virginia Tech is by catching kids before they feel so alienated they want to kill their classmates. It goes right back to Johann Hari's proposed antidote for so many mental health woes: connection. Disconnection means you feel as though you have nothing to lose. Disconnection means the world can burn, because there's nothing left in it that you hold dear. If you are not connected to the people around you, you will not be invested in their well-being. You will not give a shit about what happens to them.

When I first heard about Columbine, I can't say I didn't imagine what it would have been like to watch the faces of people who had mocked you shrink away in terror. When I first accessed the dark web, I can't say I didn't look up guns out of curiosity. It's easy to say now that I would never have done anything, but what if things had been worse? My life wasn't particularly difficult. I had a couple of friends, though they tended to keep their distance after I started devoting most of my free time to getting drunk and high with older kids from worse schools. But what if I'd had none at all? What if YouTube had already switched on its algorithm for showing viewers increasingly fucked-up videos? What if I'd inadvertently found online friends who admired and idolized school shooters?

I had anger to spare. Anger at being denied the perceived privilege of normality. Anger at not being the confident, sporty kid who everyone looked up to and liked. Anger at being forced to sit, day after day, in an ugly building filled with shitheads who didn't like you, who might decide to choke you on your way home from school while gutting your pockets of any change you'd saved by skipping lunch. Though it's fairly obvious Sam had been planning a school shooting, if I'd ordered a gun to empty my skull with, I think the police might have come to the same conclusion. I had googled most school shooters, after all, plus I had a printout of *The Anarchist Cookbook*, kindly donated by a friend, which consisted of around four hundred pages of detailed instructions for making explosives, drilling replica weapons, and committing credit card fraud. I also had the album *Holy Wood* by Marilyn Manson.

Eric Harris and Dylan Klebold, the two perpetrators of the Columbine massacre, were initially believed to have been at least partly motivated by the music of Marilyn Manson. With lyrics about violence, gore, despair, and death, he was an easy enough scapegoat, and despite the two teenage murderers having hated his music, the association stuck. In his 2002 documentary, *Bowling for Columbine*, Michael Moore asked Manson – whose real name is, somewhat disappointingly, Brian – what he would have said to the students at Columbine and the wider community. He replied, 'I wouldn't have said a single word to them. I would listen to what they have to say. And that's what no one did.'

VI

How do you order a gun on the dark web? I'm sure the more panic prone amongst you are desperate to find out. After all, if your son or daughter decides to order a Kalashnikov, you'll need your own weapon to take them out (at least this seems to be the logic behind American gun law). So I'll give you a brief rundown.

The dark web is part of the internet you can't get to in the normal way. You do not get to it, as my mum believed, through inadvertently clicking on shady-looking cartoon porn pop-ups. You have to download a specific browser, like Tor, whose icon is a little purple onion. That browser will allow you to access an encrypted network that can't be reached via the familiar portals of Chrome or Firefox.

It is not illegal to do this. And is not exclusively used as a way of doing illegal things. For many users, Tor is just a way to browse the internet in complete privacy and total security. It is used by activist groups, whistle-blowers, and a branch of the US navy. It also provides access to a number of marketplaces where, amongst other things (steroids, stolen credit card details, fake money, fake IDs, fake gift vouchers, and real weapons), drugs can be purchased. To find the addresses for such marketplaces, you can simply search the normal, friendly, it-came-with-the-computer web. There you'll find long strings of letters and numbers that can be cut and pasted into your purple onion.

Items are purchased with bitcoin on dark web marketplaces. Possibly the funniest beneficiary of the bitcoin boom was the rapper 50 Cent, who was in the midst of a bankruptcy trial when he found an old hard drive containing a fair chunk of the cryptocurrency he'd earned while trialling it as a means of payment for merchandise and then promptly forgotten about. The contents of the hard drive were sold on for sixteen million dollars. The price of bitcoin has since fallen dramatically. At the time of writing, it's hovering around six thousand dollars per coin.

I also had a pre-boom bitcoin wallet on an old computer but failed to recover it. If I had, I doubt I'd be spending my time writing this book right now.

VII

A child who feels ridiculed by their peers, ignored by the opposite gender, and belittled by teachers, may eventually learn that
Columbine took place, and discover that its perpetrators are
now hailed as heroes on some far-out islands of the internet. In
the same way that twenty-somethings working dead-end jobs
have been lured to go and fight for ISIS, the promise of power
for the powerless can be incredibly dangerous. The desire for
control and revenge, together with factors like a society that
is increasingly unlikely to make a distinction between fame
and infamy, are the most commonly advanced explanations
for the actions of school shooters: disconnection, discontent,
powerlessness, inspiration, and a desire for notoriety.

But a plane will usually only crash if a great number of small
things go wrong. Many safety checks have to fail, impeccably
maintained equipment has to malfunction, and multiple humans
have to fuck up if a Boeing jet is going to face-plant the ocean.
There is no single mistake that can knock a commercial aero-
plane out of the sky. In the same way, no one thing will reliably
set a kid on course to do something as horrific as Columbine.
Eric Harris and Dylan Klebold did not begin life with a plan to
shoot up their school. They started out committing acts of petty
vandalism and pissing about with fireworks. They were taken to
court after breaking into a van and stealing equipment from it.
I can imagine that the more these small offences mount up, the
more you begin to feel separated from others. The more you may

begin to adopt an 'us vs them' mentality. The more fractured your relationship with your parents and family may become. Things spiral out of control.

I know that after my first major fuck-up – hospitalization for drinking at thirteen – many more followed in quick succession. I no longer cared about getting in trouble, I no longer cared about what my parents thought, and I no longer cared very much about myself. If you've done something once, you're more likely to keep hitting the 'fuck-it button', especially if the punishment felt crippling or isolating. You've already broken trust and been labelled as delinquent, so you have less and less to lose.

The point of talking about school shooters in this book is not because your child is likely to become one, but because no one is likely to become one, and yet some still do. If your kid goes missing in a forest, you race to find them before they become lost in its depths. You try to catch them before they've gone too far in to hear you calling their name. You know there are parts of that forest that will be impenetrable to you. You know that if your child wanders in too far alone they'll end up somewhere dark and inescapable.

The key protection against this is the connection I've already mentioned: connection with parents, connection with peers, and connection with the institution that is educating them. One of my favourite ideas of connection is found in the work of Kurt Vonnegut, who, in his 1963 book *Cat's Cradle*, creates a religion named Bokononism. One of the teachings of this religion is that we will each find ourselves belonging to two different kinds of groups throughout our lives:

- A granfalloon is a meaningless association of human beings that many people fail to realize is meaningless. For example, being born in the same country or having been to the same university as someone else and believing that because of this, you have something in common. School is a granfalloon* for all but the most confident 1 per cent of its kids.
- A karass, on the other hand, is a group consisting of your true people. Where a granfalloon is the people who are forced upon you, a karass is the people you choose to stick with. You may find them by accident but you keep them around by choice. These are the people that you are capable of forming real bonds with. These are the people it is most difficult to find.

In 2016 the American writer, Michael Chabon, wrote a piece for *GQ* titled 'My Son, the Prince of Fashion'. He described how his twelve-year-old son, Abe, started showing signs of being different to other kids from a young age. Not only that, Abe revelled in his difference. He carefully curated his own outfits the night before going to school and would confidently wear extravagant clothes while standing on the streets of their neighbourhood. Chabon spoke about how his son inevitably received taunts and jeers from his peers for how he dressed.

The article hinges on the writer taking Abe to Paris Fashion

---

* This has not been given a squiggly red underline, which is nice. I can only imagine that the creator of Microsoft Word was a Vonnegut fan.

Week. There, he becomes tired of staring at pouting models and allows his son to go to a show with a group of men involved in the fashion industry. His son returns beaming madly.

A few days later, when it becomes time to fly home, Abe becomes curiously melancholy and starts saying that he desperately doesn't want to leave France. It doesn't take Chabon long to figure out why. 'Abe had not been dressing up, styling himself, for all these years because he was trying to prove how different he was from everyone else,' he writes. 'He did it in the hope of attracting the attention of somebody else – somewhere, someday – who was the same. He was not flying his freak flag; he was sending up a flare, hoping for rescue, for company in the solitude of his passion.'

Most young fashionistas won't have famous dads to escort them to glitzy events, so this is where the internet steps in. If you love ferrets and know no one else at school who shares your passion, you can spend long nights online, in the company of those who do understand you. These people become your people. You find somewhere you belong, somewhere to vent your fears and frustrations, and form bonds and connections by listening to the fears and frustrations of others. But this also goes for someone who hasn't been lucky enough to discover a passion. If you have no friends at school and spend your nights aimlessly trawling the blue-lit corridors of the outer web, you might stumble onto something less savoury than ferrets, and it might offer you a darker story, meaning, and sense of power.

As a teenager, you need somewhere to belong. Whether this is the annals of 4chan, the pantheon of school shooters, or something markedly more wholesome, will be down to the opportunities you're afforded and the kind of identification you're looking for. Angry kids are likely to seek out other angry kids. Depressed teens often seek out other depressed teens. A large part of finding a group, though, can be pure chance. Maybe you see a video of James Galway playing the flute and from that day on you devote every waking moment to perfecting your scales so you can thrive in the Royal Philharmonic Orchestra. Or maybe, instead, you see a video of alt-right extremists blaming Muslim immigrants for sex crimes and this becomes your *raison d'être*, and the banner beneath which you meet your closest pals. At my most lost, I found a book in a second-hand bookshop that read unlike anything I'd read before. The sentences were short and blunt. The main character did nothing. And there were no paragraphs. From there, I looked up the writer online and found that he existed in an international online community of writers that shared work, published each other, and spent long nights on group video chats talking about nothing in particular. The publisher of that book would go on to become my first publisher. Many of the writers in that circle went on to become friends in the real world.

These things are important, not just to young people but to everyone. There are hundreds of books written about the importance of community, of working together towards common goals, as we humans are supposed to do. School, as much as it would like to, does not generally constitute a community but a collection of communities. Students don't work together for a common goal, except in the odd project or homework assignment. Generally they work for themselves and for their own academic advancement. School does, however, offer plenty of opportunities for community. I don't think it's any coincidence that we imagine sporty kids to be the most confident, and I don't think their confidence comes entirely from their athletic abilities. Being part of a team, whether that team is aiming to score goals or reach the moon, is beneficial to all of us*.

Although they're often told that they're the most mollycoddled generation in history, Generation Z's rates of stress, loneliness, and depression are higher than those of their predecessors. This stress and depression make them perfect potential converts to extremist ideas and groups that offer purpose and belonging. Everyone must belong somewhere. It is up to parents to make sure that somewhere is not a very dark place.

Don't forget:

- You need to be able to trust that your teenager isn't looking at things online that could have a negative impact on the way they think. You will not be able to do this by checking their internet history.
- Pay attention to what your teenagers are watching on YouTube. Pay even more attention to the ideas that they're being exposed to online.
- History can be deleted but, if they had any sense, a

---

* A 2018 review by Andersen, Ottesen, and Thing of Copenhagen University Hospital looked at seventeen studies and found consistent evidence that, regardless of age, sport, or mental health problems, playing team sports improved social and psychological health. It's not a mind-blowing discovery.

teenager would store the bitcoin necessary to buy anything from dark web sites in an offline wallet somewhere
on their computer. They'd probably have renamed this
something innocuous, but you might stumble across it.
Also look for the little purple onion of the Tor browser
on their desktop. If you're really set on doing detective
work, these might be clues that lead somewhere.

Homework:

Go to 4chan.net/b/. This is the best-known board on the site.
It's the birthplace of most of 4chan's controversies, including the
celebrity nude leak scandal. If you're feeling brave, try posting
something and see what people have to say in response. I'm sure
they'll be kind.

Lesson Five:

Thoughtlessness is Now a Crime

Online justice, cancel culture, and critical thinking

I

'EVERYONE SHUT THE FUCK UP,' tweeted Naomi. 'I GOT ACCEPTED FOR A NASA INTERNSHIP.'

'Language,' tweeted back renowned scientist Homer Hickham, whose avatar was of an innocuous looking older man dressed in a blazer.

'Suck my dick and balls,' replied Naomi. 'I'm working at NASA.'

'And I am on the National Space Council that oversees NASA,' answered Homer.

Thus, Naomi's internship at NASA ended before it even started. Notably, it wasn't Homer himself who had it cancelled – he later explained that he was a Vietnam vet and hadn't found her tweets offensive in the slightest – but NASA, who felt forced to do something after the series of tweets went viral and hundreds of thousands of people decided to mock and demean Naomi.

The lesson is clear. One seemingly minor slip-up from the comfort of your bedroom can have devastating real-world consequences. Justice can be doled out swiftly and disproportionately. You never know which tweets, snapchats or Instagram posts will end up being presented to the baying court of online jurors. You never know when you will close your laptop only for your phone to start buzzing with news of a life turned upside down.

II

Young people themselves are taking to the role of prosecutors with glee. Many have such a keenly felt sense of right and wrong that they find doling out judgement both easy and satisfying. Sometimes, this can be a force for great change and good. Other times, it can descend into something that becomes indistinguishable from bullying.

Imagine that a hypothetical young man has just entered his third year of secondary school. In a lesson on biology, he raises his clammy hand and proposes that women shouldn't play rugby.

'They're lovely,' he stutters. 'But they're different to men so maybe they should do different things.'

The class is, rightfully, aghast.*

---

* I witnessed this exact situation recently in a language class of eighteen-to-twenty-four-year-olds. A man who had recently emigrated from Iran tried to explain, in very shitty B1-level German, that he thought women had different roles than men. For the rest of the course, he was avoided, shunned, and gossiped about as though he were an irredeemable tyrant. This inability or unwillingness to take context or complexity into account is divisive and corrosive.

'You're a misogynist,' someone says.

'I am not,' responds our imaginary boy, bewildered. 'I love women.'

'You only love their butts,' shouts someone.

'You deserve to die!' shouts someone else.

(Perhaps exaggerated for the classroom, but reasonably tame for the internet.)

'All right,' says the teacher. 'Let's all calm down.'

'Miss, he thinks women aren't people.'

'That's not what I said.'

Clearly, the boy has an outdated, harmful point of view, but what is the best course of action here? Let's assume, for the sake of argument, that he inherited this view from his parents, who inherited it from their parents, in a society that has long been structured around men. There is almost definitely no spite or malice behind the boy's view, just an acceptance that this is the way things are, because it's the way he's been taught things are.

We want to change his mind. We want him to realize why he's wrong, so that he can go forth into the world and treat women with the respect and dignity they deserve. But has anyone ever changed their mind after being shouted at? Has anyone ever changed their mind after being wilfully misunderstood and publicly shamed?

We know this is not how things work, or how things get better, but it is increasingly the way we respond to such misdemeanours. Rather than offer empathy or understanding, we fight with fire, and we're not even fighting fire with fire – most of the time we're fighting a spent match with a flamethrower. We opt for immediate

condemnation. We do not think that perpetrators deserve understanding, patience, or second chances. We do not think it is our
responsibility to explain to the boy how harmful the shit he's
spouting might be. He should know better, he should be better,
but he is not, and so he will be punished.

The boy's roasting probably will not end once the bell rings.
In corridors and classrooms, he will be harangued.

'Misogynist,' people will spit at him during lunch break.

'What the fuck is wrong with you?' his peers will ask.

Maybe the boy will try to explain that he made a mistake, he
was speaking without thinking, that he's watched some Roxane
Gay videos on YouTube since and knows better now. But it's too
late. For this kind of shaming, there is hardly any mechanism in
place for redemption. We are less open than ever to the idea that
people can change. Criminals are quietly released from prison for
murder, but a comedian who makes an ill-timed joke might find
themselves spending eternity in the stocks.

If your child had been one of those hounding our hypothetical
misogynist, are you proud of them for standing up against him,
or have they taken it too far? At what point has it gone too far?
Is it still standing up against something if everyone else is on
your side? Is there any point in standing up in a situation where
condemnation, rather than enlightenment, is the goal? When
does condemnation become bullying? When, if ever, is bullying
justified?

And does it matter? Because regardless of the nuances, it's clear
that at some point most kids are likely to find themselves on one
side of the seesaw or the other. They will either get something

wrong and be hounded for it, or join in the piling-on of someone else who has got something wrong.

The idea of an unbridled mob sounds disturbing, and it can be, but this unbridled mob can often find justice where traditional means have failed. What has changed most recently is that for the first time young people can and do use the internet to effect real change by calling out their peers as well as adults in a public forum. When, in the past, could a fourteen-year-old pull up someone three times her age for dead-naming* a trans person? When could a sixteen-year-old boy rally an army of thousands against a drinks company for their misjudged attempt to cash in on social justice?

We've seen this again and again in #MeToo cases. The legal system lets women down, so they seek the justice they deserve by another means. They stand up and speak out about their experiences and the experiences of others who have been silenced. Powerful, cruel men are toppled. As the police sit by twiddling their thumbs, the villagers have taken up their pitchforks and driven the monsters out of town.

This is one side of the coin of online vigilante justice. On the other, an older woman who inadvertently uses the incorrect pronoun for a trans person is bawled at until she abandons the internet. A scientist who wears a shirt with female bodies on it (gifted to him by a female colleague) is harassed to the point of a sobbing apology in the days after his team announce a startling

---

* Calling a trans person by the name they were assigned at birth rather than the name they have chosen for themselves.

breakthrough. An academic who tells the button-pusher in a lift that the floor they want is 'ladies' lingerie' is let go by the university he's given decades of his life to. A care worker who poses jokily in front of Arlington National Cemetery is sacked and finds it impossible to get another job.

The internet will encourage you to condemn the villain of the day. It doesn't matter how hapless or helpless this villain might be. The distance and depersonalization created by the internet can turn us into unrecognizable monsters. When it comes to justice on the internet, the temptation is to treat humans who have come down on the wrong side of an issue as though they are the living embodiment of racism, misogyny, or transphobia, rather than living, breathing human beings. When commenters write 'I hope you die' in response to a tweet, it's as though they're not talking to the forty-five-year-old Glaswegian who wore blackface to her friend's party ten years ago – they're talking to racism itself. That, I think, seems to be the only way of understanding why otherwise normal people spout such vitriol.

My little brother recently told me he'd stopped watching a YouTuber he'd previously enjoyed.

'He's cancelled,' he explained.

'What does that mean?'

'We don't like him any more. His videos are stupid.'

'Why?'

'He said something mean.'

'About who?'

'Another YouTuber.'

There's something strangely sad to me about thinking that way.

The willingness to dispose of people when they put a foot wrong doesn't feel like a step in the right direction. If we're now subject to a court without laws, in which anyone can join the jury, it's inevitable that punishments will be doled out unfairly. Imagine treating your family that way:

Dad: Right, we're just off to Sally's dressing-up party.

Oscar: Wait, what's that on your head?

Dad: It's a headdress, like Indians wear.

Oscar: Firstly, it's racist to call them Indians. Secondly, that's cultural appropriation. That headdress is a symbol of an oppressed culture, not part of your costume.

Dad: It's just a bit of fun, Osc.

Oscar: You're cancelled.

Dad: I'm what?

Oscar: You're fired from your job.

Dad: I'm not fired from my job.

Oscar: You are. I called your boss and he doesn't want to have to deal with negative publicity around you being such a massive racist.

Dad: I'm not a racist!

Oscar: Tell that to all the friends I've invited over to throw things at your racist head.

Dad: Oscar, what is going on?

Oscar: I am never going to talk to or listen to you ever again.

Dad: But—

Oscar: You are no longer my father.

What has happened to our sense of proportion, and what does it mean for the way that kids will judge themselves and each other? How do we keep young people from believing that joining forces to demolish a person's life is the appropriate response to catching them in a mistake? Especially when they watch it happen day after day on the internet. We seem to have dispensed entirely with the notion of treating others as we'd like to be treated ourselves, partly because people are becoming unable to imagine themselves in the shoes of others. But if young people continue to perpetuate this system of disproportionate justice, they may very well one day find themselves becoming the victims of it. And if your child ever finds themselves on the wrong side of this kind of online campaign, it will already be too late.

III

Invisibilia is a wonderful and popular NPR podcast created by the American producers Hanna Rosin and Alix Spiegel. They tend to pull apart various thoughts, feelings, and behaviours until you're left scratching your head about even the most basic building blocks of being a human.

At the time of writing, their last episode was titled 'The End of Empathy'. It revolved around the story of an ex-incel who had since claimed to have changed for the better, leaving behind his passion of calling women cunts in chat rooms for good.

The producers sent a new young colleague off to investigate, presuming she would come back with a story of epiphany and redemption. This is not what she came back with. She put together a piece questioning the ex-incel's narrative and asking whether he really deserved a chance to simply repent, apologize, and move forward. A key piece of the puzzle was a decades-long piece of research conducted by Harvard University. In the course of the study, surveys were given to cross sections of college and high school students from the late sixties on. The surveys remained the same and included statements that students were asked to rate the truthfulness of. These included assertions like 'I sometimes find it difficult to see things from the other guy's point of view', 'I try to look at everybody's side of a disagreement before I make a decision', and 'I often have tender, concerned feelings for people less fortunate than me.' As the podcast reported, the study found all forms of empathy starting to fall amongst students from the year 2000. By 2009, the average young person reported being 40 percent less empathetic than the previous generation.

It might be a startling statistic but it can't be surprising when you see the roughness with which those who fall out of favour are dealt with.

The majority of people under twenty rejoiced when the far-right Australian senator had an egg broken over his head, turning the egger into an online celebrity named 'egg boy'. They applauded when Tommy Robinson had a milkshake thrown over him. They cheered when Richard Spencer was punched in the face, kick-starting a series of memes about the dire need to assault proponents of the far right. Essays with titles like 'Why Punching Nazis Is Not Only Ethical, But Imperative' sprung up around the internet. It was widely agreed that punching Nazis was fine, because the rhetoric they espouse is so dangerous, and their beliefs so unbending, that physical violence is the only reasonable response.

On one level, you can't help but feel satisfied at the image of a smug bigot being whacked out of his hate-filled reverie while doing a piece to camera beside a crumbling Debenhams. On another, you probably feel that something about it isn't quite right. Morally, this can't be where we stand. It's not a justifiable position. Where does it end? Do we start tracking down bigamists and giving them wedgies? Tripping up tax dodgers? Clotheslining* carnivores? When is a belief a reasonable point of view and when is it something that warrants a person having a lasagne thrown over them every time they nip out for a pint of milk?

The problem is not so much with the extremists – I struggle to summon any sympathy for racist men being doused in junk food – but with this refusal to think rationally about the aims of this kind of behaviour. Does someone punching a Nazi really think it will change something? Or is this another case of them knowing that it will be filmed, like-minded people will cheer them on, and they will revel in the positive feedback? Is it the equivalent of sending an 'End Racism Now' image to your sixteen, vehemently anti-racist followers because you know they'll click 'like' on it? What is the point? What are you hoping to achieve?

In his book, *So You've Been Publicly Shamed*, Jon Ronson investigates the case of Justine Sacco. Justine was the PR

---

* Holding out your arm so that someone runs into it at neck-level. Clotheslining is considered a move in wrestling and a foul in football.

consultant who, before climbing on a plane bound for Cape Town, tweeted: 'Going to Africa. Hope I don't get AIDS. Just kidding, I'm white!' By the time her plane had landed, the tweet had been seen by millions of people. Thousands of them had tweeted about Justine being a bitch, a cunt, a racist, and someone deserving of a slow and painful death. She had also been fired from her job.

As Jon Ronson points out, it's hard to believe that anyone who read the tweet really thought she was being racist. It was a joke, not a really funny one, but not a really racist one either. It hinges on the idea that white people do not believe things like AIDS will happen to them. It does not hinge on the idea that Justine Sacco thinks white people can't get AIDS or that she genuinely is at some risk while being in Africa.

Still, the machinery of online judgement jolted into action and pulled Justine's life out from under her. Few people would suggest that professionals ought to lose their livelihoods over bad jokes, but we exist at a time when it happens again and again. And it isn't just faceless basement-dwelling trolls who participate. Otherwise sane celebrities join these pile-ons of the powerless; accountants from rural Idaho or art school students with sixty Twitter followers are furiously torn apart by the pack of digital wolves, crusading for justice. No one is given a chance to explain themselves and no explanations are listened to. We no longer look for nuance. Someone is either bad and not deserving of anything, or good and deserving of the world. As Obama pointed out at his 2019 Obama Foundation summit, it seems that increasing numbers of young people believe, 'the way of me making change is by being as judgemental as possible about other people.'

I was once very kindly offered the diagnosis of borderline personality disorder. Having by then become disillusioned with the idea of tacking letters onto the end of my name, I declined, but there is one trait of BPD that helps makes sense of the phenomenon: 'a pattern of intense and unstable relationships characterized by alternating between extremes of idealization and devaluation.' This is the perfect summary of the so-called 'cancel culture' that has come to dominate social media. We tend to see people as either perfect or worthless: you are either Jeff Goldblum or Roseanne Barr, Greta Gerwig or Scarlett Johansson, Ariana Grande or Lena Dunham. You are either a wonderful, beautiful, talented person or a steaming bag of irredeemable dog shit. And this can change in a second. One ill-thought-out comment will boot you from one column to the other. As a celebrity, you may fall asleep a hero and wake up a villain.

We reserve our empathy for those we like, and judge those we don't without understanding. But by reserving empathy for the ones we care about, all we're really doing is insulating ourselves. The unexpectedness of Brexit and Trump were both down to failures of empathy. The majority of online liberals refused to empathize with people who thought differently to them, refused to believe in the beliefs of others, and were catastrophically blind-sided because of it.

This is the context in which young people are coming of age. This is the kind of black-and-white morality they are being exposed to and absorbing through the internet. You either espouse the correct points of view and are clapped on the back, or mutter the wrong ones and are ostracized and shouted down, possibly to such an extent that you end up moping in the dingy corners of 4chan, learning about how lizards killed Brittany Murphy and it is the fault of shallow women and Jews that you've never got laid. The internet is not built to foster genuine conversation and dialogue, but to whip us into frenzies of righteous fury. The only way to resist is to cultivate the ability to think independently.

The most vital and long-impacting aspect of school was, for me, A level critical thinking. This was where we learned how to recognize fallacies, deconstruct arguments, and discern when you are being manipulated, distracted, or lied to. At the beginning of our first lesson, a teacher stood at the front and promised that what we were about to learn would constitute the most important element of our school education. Everyone rolled their eyes. But she was right. Years later, when I talk to schoolfriends, we tend to agree that critical thinking is the one subject that we still employ, day after day, especially in the current climate.

During one early lesson we were shown an advert for a shampoo which, for legal reasons, I'll call No'Real. In the advert, a conventionally attractive woman with a silky mane of chestnut hair stared down a camera and whispered, 'Studies show that the majority of women prefer No'Real to other shampoos.'

'What's the advert saying?' our teacher asked.

'It's better than other shampoos,' someone said.

'Could she be lying?'

'You're not allowed to lie in adverts,' someone else piped up, smugly.

'So No'Real is better than other shampoos?'

It seemed like a trick question. No one knew what to say. The teacher then directed our attention to the small print of the advert: 'Out of a study of twelve women, seven preferred No'Real to the other brands tested.' Aside from the fact that this sample size was much too small to draw any conclusions from, we were told, it didn't mention the other brands tested, meaning they might have been compared to dog shampoo, Asda Smartprice armpit wash, and Colman's mayonnaise.

'How dare they!' we crowed.

Everyone was outraged and we all vowed never to use No'Real again.

This is a straightforward case of looking a bit closer at supporting evidence, but we were also introduced to logical fallacies, like straw man arguments, in which rather than respond directly to the claim of an opponent, an attacker rages against an exaggerated, distorted, tangentially related position.

For example, let's say Oscar asks his mum if he can please stay out until eleven with his friends.

'No,' she says. 'That's far too late. You might get mugged or meet a witch.'

'So you don't want me to ever have any fun?'

'No, I do want you to have fun.'

'But I would have fun if you let me go out and you aren't letting me go out so obviously you don't want me to have any fun.'

Or, in politics, some kindly American may suggest banning guns in schools, to which someone else might reply, 'You want to stop Americans carrying guns? You literally want to change the constitution.'

'No, that's not what I want.'

'So you agree we should, as the constitution claims, be able to carry guns?'

'Yes.'

'Well, then. I think we can all agree I've won this argument and we can move on to talking about less ridiculous ideas.'

Straw men push us away from talking with subtlety. They are used to distract us from real, difficult issues by obscuring them with more straightforward ones. They were leaned on heavily by both sides of the Brexit campaign, with ripostes such as, so you don't ever want to go on holiday? You hate brown people? You think that bananas are supposed to be straight? They have also found their way into the rhetoric used to 'cancel' people who make what ought to be considered forgivable mistakes in full view of the global internet.

Once certain logical fallacies have been brought to your attention, it's difficult to stop spotting them. Like a lonely singleton seeing in-love couples on every street corner, once my critical thinking class had learned the names of fallacies, we began seeing them everywhere.

If your son or daughter ever gets the chance to study it, I recommend that you sit down with them and seriously consider taking critical thinking. It has helped me immeasurably. Now I read the tiny print at the bottom of shampoo adverts, distinguish between attacks on people and attacks on their beliefs, and can recognize the tactics that politicians constantly employ to divert attention away from issues that really matter. If I had any of the relevant power, I would make critical thinking a mandatory part of education. Before sex or religion or the Tudors, your kid needs to be taught how to evaluate the unending barrage of information the internet delivers to their bedrooms.

IV

As we saw in chapter 3, it isn't only things you might say today, but things you've said or done in the distant past that could be dragged before the online courtroom. Kevin Hart lost his job hosting the Oscars as a result of an eight-year-old tweet in which he expressed homophobic views. James Gunn, the creator of the incredibly lucrative *Guardians of the Galaxy*, was sacked from the third film for years-old tweets joking about rape.

After one of my books did better than expected, I was advised to comb through old tweets and delete anything that could reflect badly in the current climate. I deleted a handful of things, mostly to do with fancying certain celebrities, one to do with asking whether a certain politician was on her period. I would not say those things now, but of course I said stupid shit when I was eighteen: I was eighteen. The idea that we should be judged not only by throwaway comments, but by throwaway comments made by our younger selves, is terrifying, and points towards a future in which no one is safe.

V

Here's the good news: as wonderful, well-rounded adults, you can help your teenagers express their feelings of injustice in more considered and effective ways.

In 2014, the eighties TV series *21 Jump Street* was remade as a film starring Channing Tatum and Jonah Hill. If you haven't seen it, I recommend you take a two-hour break from reading this and come back later. If you don't have time: the plot revolves around two recent recruits to the police as they are sent undercover to a high school in order to try and get to the bottom of who has been distributing a potent new drug called HFS (holy fucking shit). Tatum plays a cool, muscular, jock-type character called Jenko, while Hill is a 'nerdy', overweight character named Schmidt.

They have different feelings about going back to school: Tatum remembers being popular and well liked, while Hill remembers being academically successful but bullied. At least they both know what to do to fit in: they need to be apathetic and rude. They also need to drive a large, gas-guzzling muscle car, which they gleefully borrow from the police and ride to school. 'Park in the disabled bay,' Hill says to Tatum as they're pulling into the car park. 'It'll make us look so cool.'

From the script:

We meet ERIC MOLSON, 18, eco-friendly,
who hangs out with AMIR, 16, some ATTRACTIVE TEENS
on CUSTOM HIPSTER BICYCLES.

ERIC

Is that your car? I saw you guys roar in this
morning. What's that get? Ten miles to the
gallon?

JENKO

(proud) Try seven. You?

Eric nods to Amir, who leans on the Mercedes,
hardcore.

AMIR

Biodiesel, dawg.

SCHMIDT

Smells like egg rolls.

ERIC

Yeah it does. Runs on leftover fry oil from
Hunan Palace. But we try to ride bikes if we
can. Global crisis and whatnot.

JENKO

Whatever, man. I don't care about anything.

Jenko winks at Schmidt. Amir steps to Eric's side,
ready to throw down.

ERIC (to Jenko)
You don't care about the environment? Kinda
fucked up, man.
Schmidt quickly backpedals.

SCHMIDT
I care about the environment. I don't flush like,
ever.

JUARIO
Guys, History test second period. I'm trying to
study, okay?

JENKO
Ha ha. He's trying! Nerd.

JUARIO
Who you calling nerd?

Juario puts the book down and steps to him.
Jenko punches Juario to the ground.

JENKO
Now turn off that gay ass music.

JUARIO
You punched me because I'm gay?

Everyone in the parking lot stops and stares.
Schmidt takes a step away from him, embar-
rassed.

JENKO

No. What? Come on.

SCHMIDT

(to Jenko) That's not cool, man.

ERIC

He's right. That is not okay.

JENKO

No! I didn't punch him because he's gay! I
punched him and he happened to be gay, afterwards.

JUARIO

I was gay when you punched me.

This sums up the shift in the dominant mode of young people:
it is no longer cool not to care, it isn't cool to be intolerant. In
the same way that smoking and moonboots have fallen out of
fashion, so have apathy and cruelty. Young people feel that they
can't afford not to care. It feels as though the planet is in trouble
and the adults are doing a terrible job of keeping the world a
sane place. Blinded by nostalgia for a time that never existed,

the caretakers of the Western world make poor decision after poor decision. In America, the adults elected a racist, bigoted, pantomime clown. In Britain, they voted to isolate themselves, lose huge amounts of industry, and cut off their own noses to spite their own stupid faces. We know climate change is going to render the planet uninhabitable for our ancestors yet we refuse to make radical change. We know that people are dying because of an underfunded NHS, yet we fail to tax some of the largest companies while they continue to hoover up our money and offer their employees all the rights of robotic limbs on production lines.

Teenagers are not waiting for out-of-touch rock stars like Bono or Bob Geldof to lead them in sickly, expensive, emotionally manipulative charity blowouts. They are doing things for themselves. If they don't do it, they're realizing, no one will. Young people might be looking at *bukkake* porn, but they're also using the internet to fight for their idea of a better world.

Greta Thunberg and her climate change talks have rocketed her into global consciousness and have managed to mobilize children in schools across 140 countries to the cause. Kids are striking in protest at the feeble measures put in place by governments to combat the disintegration of our planet. Of course, I thought, they're 'striking' because it means a day off – a view echoed on panel shows and radio debates across Britain. But I was mistakenly thinking like Channing Tatum's character. The truth is, a lot of teenagers care. They care about the environment, about LGBTQ freedoms, and about human rights. They are the most liberal, tolerant generation yet to complain about curfews. And these beliefs aren't those of a fringe movement, like the hippies, they are the norm. They are so important that the face of capitalism is changing in their likeness.

Pepsi clumsily tried to make itself relevant through an advert in which a bottle of sugary brown liquid peacefully ended a protest that bore more than a passing resemblance to recent Black Lives Matter demonstrations. Stella Artois is luring in a generation of new drinkers by pledging a month of water to a family in the developing world for every limited-edition bottle bought. Nike hired Colin Kaepernick for an ad campaign after he flouted rules by taking a knee during the national anthem in protest at systemic racism. Airbnb ran an advert during the height of the Syrian refugee crisis about how 'No matter who you are, where you're from, who you love, or who you worship, you deserve to belong.' And as I'm writing, Burger King has just been pilloried for an ad campaign related to mental health, part of which has involved the launch of 'unhappy meals'.

Even social media sites try to remain relevant by positioning themselves on the right side of this recent re-emergence of activism. It's my birthday in a few days, Facebook suggested: 'It's almost your birthday! Why not set up a fundraiser for a cause you admire and have all your friends donate? We will not even ask for a donation processing fee.' Even the big blue behemoth of social media wants you to think it's unselfish and committed to social change.

The switch in tactics of advertisers from 'drink this to be cool' to 'drink this to save the planet' is proof enough that what young people want most of all is change. If it didn't shift products, corporations wouldn't bother to pursue it. Violent games, videos, porn, are all distractions from the fact that, for better or for worse, most young people have a keener sense of right and wrong than ever. They are less focused on wanting to be hip and more committed to wanting to be good.

Just for a second, between the school shootings and the abundance of niche porn, I'd like to express a sense of hope for the generation you're currently raising. At the very least, many of them care – about the planet and about each other – and this is a real reason to hold on to hope that humanity isn't necessarily doomed to the grimy, violent dystopias that so many films and books have predicted. *Mad Max* may not be inevitable. Our grandchildren may never have to fight to tear out each other's throats in *The Hunger Games*.

VI

The main takeaway from all this is to be careful. The world has become less forgiving. In its attempt to right wrongs, it has, in many areas, begun to overcorrect. Teens need to look after themselves, and parents need to teach them how to do that. For the time being at least, this is the way things are, and there's little sign of them changing. Punishments meted out by the internet bear little relation to crimes, or even the law, and they can have impacts that extend far longer than jail sentences. If the first page of Google results for your kid's name becomes polluted by some form of scandal, future employers will see, future friends and lovers will see, and their life will be difficult.

It's become clear that teenagers should try to refrain from telling all but their closest friends to suck their dick and balls on the internet, no matter how enjoyable it might be to say. A good strategy employed by a number of people I know is to maintain two accounts on certain sites. One account is locked (so that only approved friends can see it) and operated under a fake name, not traceable to their real one. This is used as a sillier, jokier, more thoughtless account, where dicks and balls can be freely licked and sucked without the risk of NASA scientists finding out or evidence being preserved for presentation to the kangaroo court of online jurors. The second account is public, tame, and well thought out. This ensures that when prospective employers go trawling the internet to check if you've been trick-or-treating in blackface or calling eleven-year-olds bonerheads, they find nothing untoward. It also helps to ensure that if you misspeak or misstep, then your mistakes aren't going to be accessible to the entire world. Your friends, you might reasonably hope, will say: maybe that's not all right, maybe you might want to think again about that one.

Mistakes made in the public arena are not easily forgiven or forgotten. And we are all now in the public arena, or at least we all have the potential to be catapulted into it. Adults ought to know better, but as a teenager you are liable to mess up. The best thing you can do is to mess up in private and make sure not to leave muddy footprints across the internet.

I dread to think about the possibility of cancel culture influencing the way that young people interact. It's something that's beyond my power to research in any meaningful way. Maybe it's had no effect at all. Maybe we won't know for sure if there has been an effect until this generation has grown up. Maybe most young people act one way on the internet and in a completely different way in real life. Even if their online behaviour isn't reflected in real-world actions, it does have real-world consequences for other human beings.

On the internet, the judgement of kids can be worth as much as the judgements of their parents, often more, given the superior skills younger people tend to have at mobilizing and expressing themselves in the digital realm. They wield power over the lives of strangers. And with great power – say it with me – comes great responsibility. Oscar could potentially discover a photo of a woman on the other side of the world and have it seen by a hundred thousand people in a few seconds.* In his rush to be seen to be on the side of good and to receive congratulations, he might share the picture and end up destroying a life. Young people have to be careful about what they distribute. They have to pause and think, not just about whether it has the potential to do them harm, but about whether it has the potential to do others harm, and whether that harm can be justified in the name of social justice.

At its inception, it was hoped that the internet would become a vehicle for true democracy, a place in which everyone could

---

* This is not, by the way, an exaggeration. Almost every friend I know with Twitter, regardless of follower count, has at least one tweet that has gone viral to some degree. One woman, who has just over eighty followers, has one tweet that was liked by over twenty thousand people. Spheres of influence are unpredictable. You never know how many people will be listening.

both speak and be heard. For the millennials who have spent their lives hopelessly wired into it, it might seem to have done little but offer another way for corporations to monetize them. For a new, more savvy generation, it might well be the means to achieving the fairer society they're striving for, provided they can keep from going mad with new-found power.

Now more than ever, young people are looking for answers. The problem is that the internet has a thousand of them, and no benevolent, objective online teacher to guide them towards the more helpful ones. This is a new responsibility but a vital one. Parents need to put in the effort to become more acquainted with what their children are doing online. Not just to steer them away from porn and snuff films, but to help them form healthy habits, be sure they're behaving like they would in the real world, and make certain that the digital world is serving them rather than the other way around.

Don't forget:

- Unless you're sure your children are never, ever going to post something in the least bit thoughtless, encourage them to keep online accounts private and/or maintain them under false names. It could save them a world of pain. Badly worded tweets can even lead to a visa for the US being denied.
- If they do have public accounts, either sit down with them and look through what they've posted, or encourage them to comb through their own histories, checking for

anything that might one day be used against them. No pictures of them standing proudly over the lions they've just shot, no mocking photographs they've taken of strangers, and no tweets suggesting Angela Merkel might be 'on the blob'.

- Teenagers increasingly want to do good. That doesn't mean they're succeeding. Every three-dimensional villain is convinced of their own cause. Only through discussion and debate can they be encouraged to think things through more properly.

- Critical thinking may not be an option at your kids' school, but there are any number of video lectures, podcasts, and articles about how to evaluate and analyse the information you're presented with on a daily basis. These strategies, once they've got their hooks in, can remain with someone for life.

Homework:

The recent Apple TV online series *The Morning Show* does a fairly interesting job of delving into the mechanics and nuances of the #MeToo movement and cancel culture. Watching something like that might act as a springboard for discussions that might otherwise be difficult to conjure out of thin air.

Interlude 2:

The Underestimated Power of Herbal Tea

This might sound out of place, but I believe very strongly in the power of warm drinks. They can help with everything from diarrhoea to cocaine comedowns. I know it seems like something a grandma would say, but I am not a grandma and you should at least try inflicting some of these on the teenagers in your life next time they need help because:

- Studies have ranked certain teas against serious medical medications. St John's wort has, for example, been shown to be as effective as antidepressants in treating minor and moderate depression.
- Hot drinks make you hot when you're cold and cold when you're hot.
- If you're holding something warm when you meet someone, you're more likely to like them.

- They are panaceas.
- They taste nice. Sort of. Once you get used to them.
- They are more interesting than water but don't contain sugar unless you insist on dumping it into them.

And tea shouldn't be restricted to the one very specific blend of Ceylon, Assam, and Kenya that we in Britain seem to have decided is the only liquid besides beer that's worth consuming. There are a thousand different ingredients that can lend your body a hand. Some can be just as effective as Nurofen or Imodium, a fraction of the price, and fun to roll between your palms. The most useful are:

Ginger
Ginger is the crown prince of all teas. It can help almost anything but its specialty is combating nausea. It can mean the difference between a vomiting hangover and a calm, TV-in-bed kind of hangover. So when your teenager next wakes up with a stomach that's revolting, tell them to slice up some ginger root and add hot water. Even if they don't like the taste, their body will. I swear.

Passionflower
This is useful for anxiety. Like, really useful. One study showed it to be at least as useful in treating generalized anxiety disorder as various benzodiazepines, without the side effects of spiralling addiction and severely painful withdrawals. Two cups a day. They can do it.

Valerian

For when they can't sleep. Don't take the teabag out and get them to drink it about an hour before they go to bed.

Camomile

Another calmer-downer.

Peppermint

This pretty much helps all digestive stomach stuff. It helps people with irritable bowel syndrome and it will help them if they have diarrhoea too. As someone who struggles with IBS, I can't help but feeling drinking copious amounts of this is preferable to getting through two packets of Imodium Instants a day.

Green

Green tea is a good, less intense source of caffeine than coffee. It's also, for some weird reason, good for weight loss.

English

English tea is the workhorse of teas. It will get them out of bed and ready for the day, without making them feel shaky and nervous like coffee.

Mega-tea

Slices of ginger, a camomile teabag, a peppermint teabag, half a spoon of honey, black pepper, and a slice of lemon. This is my own recipe and can cure many ailments. Either that or it tastes like a very convincing placebo.

Unless someone is feeling one hundred per cent perfect, they should go and make tea. A fully stocked tea cupboard can help a lot of things, and more importantly for this book it can sometimes do a very good job of taking the edge off a bad day. And coming to believe that a cup of something warm between your hands is going to cheer you up is enough to cheer you up in itself. If you teach young people to believe in the power of warm drinks, then warm drinks will have the power to help them.

Lesson Six:

It's Not Beer,
but It's Not Certain Death

Alcohol, drugs, self-medication, the law,
and exciting things that come in the post

I

Chances are, your teenager will, at some point, at least consider putting something mind-altering into their nose, mouth, or anus.[*]

There are two new ways of procuring drugs in the modern age. Both were impossible a decade ago; both have their own distinct advantages.

One is through the dark web, which we've already covered. The benefit of dark web marketplaces is that each item will be reviewed by other consumers, much like readers give their opinions about books on Amazon. Whether it's crack, LSD, heroin or whatever,

---

[*] Possibly not in their anus.

it will come with honest assessments to ensure that you receive nothing but the best product to suit your needs.

If I was looking for a gram of cocaine, I would select 'stimulants' from the category list and scroll through pages of pictures, typically showing a sample of the batch in front of a piece of paper showing the vendor's name to prove its source. If I saw something I liked, I'd click on it and read the reviews:

- Flaky but not overly strong. Slightly sweet drip.
- Tested at 60 per cent pure. Ordered 6g. Fine for the price.
- Slightly yellowish tinge? Tasted fine.

That sounds like a reasonable product at a reasonable price, I'd think, putting in an order for 1g. I would then pay in some form of untraceable cryptocurrency, probably bitcoin, which would be held in escrow by the website and released to the vendor only once I'd received my drugs.

My cocaine would then arrive in the post. It would not arrive in a black box marked 'drugs'. It would come in a package specifically made to look like it could contain anything other than drugs. For example, the stamp on the front might say 'Tony's eBay Computer Part Shop' or 'Booksville Poetry Books'. The drugs would be vacuum sealed and stashed inside a DVD case or a book or whatever else your dark-web dealer had lying around their flat.

This retail model is not just beneficial to getting high, it saves lives because you know which ingredients are in your drugs. People who know the strength and content of their drugs tend not to overdose on them. Two of the highest-profile deaths to hit people under twenty in 2018 – the rappers Mac Miller and Lil Peep – were both the result of accidental fentanyl ingestion; fentanyl being a super-high-strength opiate often mixed with other drugs to boost their potency, thus making them cheaper to produce. Last year, almost all major dark web drug suppliers banned the sale of fentanyl. It makes you wonder, are these the good guys or the bad guys? What are we really doing by arresting them? In any event, it seems like a waste of time going after them. Ross Ulbricht, aka Dread Pirate Roberts, the founder of the first and largest dark web marketplace, is currently serving a double life sentence without the possibility of parole. But after his website was seized and shut down, ten more sprang up. When they were forcibly closed, a hundred more took their place.

Truly, it's a wonderful system. With the arrival of the dark web, I no longer had to call unpredictable phone numbers, wait around in the cold, and nervously climb into the back seat of a Mercedes in order to buy an incredibly expensive little sachet of Persil Non Bio.

One downside to the dark web is that an order invariably takes some time to arrive. Not a lot of time, but time. It also requires a certain degree of knowledge and patience: I had to find out how to buy and transfer bitcoin, access the dark web, and be confident that my parents weren't going to insist on rifling through my post.

Enter Snapchat, an app present on the phone of almost every single under-eighteen-year-old around the globe. This is one of the more popular modern ways of sourcing drugs. The privacy settings of Snapchat makes it very useful for selling illicit goods because of the messages disappearing as soon as you've read them.

A teen will have a number of dealers and, every now and again, these dealers will brazenly send out mass messages, showing pictures of whatever it is they have on offer, along with price lists. The teen will reply with a list of what they need and the dealer will be round in half an hour. The benefit to the user is convenience. It's not foolproof, but it's an improvement on previous methods of picking up.

Where once drugs were difficult to come by, and limited to coke, weed, speed, and crap pills, they are now only a few taps away, and almost any compound you can think of is available for purchase. For a teenager looking to try that thing they heard about on *Breaking Bad*, this is great news. For the doctors who have to treat overdoses of drugs they can't identify, it can prove a nightmare.

II

The only way to make drugs safer is, predictably, through education, and young people are increasingly likely to educate themselves. There are a number of 'vaults' – most notably Erowid and Bluelight – on the internet filled with thousands of 'trip reports' in which people report exactly how much of a certain drug they took, how long the effects took to kick in, what the effects were, and whether or not it was moreish. For someone who is about to try something for the first time, these sites are incredibly useful. They also offer practical drug-safety advice such as which combinations of drugs are reasonably harmless and which can be lethal.

I once found a tiny electronic scales in a friend's bedroom and was told that it was for weighing ketamine.

'I'm not sure you should be selling ketamine,' I said.

'It's not for selling it, it's so I know how much I'm taking each time.'

Gone are the days when children can be told 'if you take drugs, you will die' and be forever scared off. They have access to the internet and, sooner or later, they'll start wondering what exactly that thing their favourite rapper keeps mumbling about is, and find out everything about it online, because it's all there.

The downside is that not everybody will be doing their research. Inevitably, without guidance, some terrifically strong drugs can wind up in the hands of some terrifically inexperienced users. For example, when I was at school a friend had a house party where a boy was hospitalized and came close to dying after snorting a line of what he thought was cocaine. It was heroin, which is far cheaper than cocaine but far more potent.

A typical first line of heroin should be this size:

-

A typical first line of cocaine might be:

_____

It's not hard to see how he wound up in trouble. But it's also not hard to see how having such a wealth of information about drugs might, in certain cases, lead kids to try things they might otherwise not have considered. Teenagers of the past have attempted to get high off banana peel and nutmeg after hearing rumours that they were capable of inducing psychedelic highs. In the modern age, you only need to conduct a quick Google search to find out neither of those methods will be particularly effective or enjoyable, though there are a number of other easily accessible ways to temporarily alter your mind.

Diphenhydramine is an antihistamine found in a number of over-the-counter sleeping pills. It is a sedative. It will get you to sleep easily but probably leave you feeling slightly groggy come the morning.

When I first read about diphenhydramine, I was eighteen years old, living with my nan and trying to find a way to make money out of writing. Most nights I drank and took plundered codeine, occasionally something more exciting. I became interested in diphenhydramine after reading trip reports in which users taking high doses reported extremely vivid hallucinations of people. I was lonely. Everyone I knew had gone to university and my girl-friend at the time lived in Scotland. Vivid hallucinations of people sounded like they might be welcome company. I was sceptical that I would specifically see other human beings, but thought it was worth a try.

I bought two packs of diphenhydramine in the form of Nytol from two separate chemists. I read the leaflets that came with them. The recommended dose for insomnia was 50mg. Most of the online trip reports had people using 400–600mg. Some were higher. I decided to use 800mg, for no reason other than being an idiot and wanting something significant to take place.

Something significant did take place.

I became fairly confused and began to feel like I was sinking. I vomited. I became disorientated. At around two in the morning, I heard a knock at the door. I answered it to find my girlfriend from Scotland had come to visit.

'You're here!' I said.

'I wanted to see you,' she replied.

It was very late, and my nan was asleep, so I whispered to her that I would just get my shoes on so we could go for a walk. When I came back from putting on my shoes, my girlfriend was gone. I panicked. I rushed into my nan's room and woke her up.

'Emma was here,' I told her.

'What are you talking about?' she said, rubbing the sleep dust out of her eyes. 'What time is it?'

I was impatient. 'Emma came to visit but she's walked off and now she's lost in the night and she doesn't know the area and we have to go and find her.'

My nan didn't look convinced. 'Why would she come at this time of night?'

'I don't know,' I said. 'But she did. Quick, we have to go and find her.'

We eventually got into the car and drove a few times round the block. 'Are you sure she was here?' she kept saying.

'Yes,' I told her.

Needless to say, we did not find Emma. We drove back home and I went to bed. As I lay on the mattress, I turned my head to find an old schoolfriend sitting on one of the pillows.

'Hello,' I remember telling him. 'I haven't seen you for a while. You're not really there, are you?'

He shook his head.

'That's okay,' I told him. 'It's nice to see you anyway.'

I woke up beside a smudge of vomit and felt like I was recovering from a car crash for days after that. In the time-honoured tradition of celebrities being assholes on planes, I told my nan I had accidentally mixed a single sleeping pill with a single beer. That is not what I had done. I had taken a close-to-lethal dose of sleeping pills because I had read about it on the internet.

So yeah, drug-experience forums can be a double-edged sword, as can almost every element of the internet.

III

Alongside ensuring that no one gets peanutted and everyone eats a bit of fruit, schools have a responsibility to offer a reasonable form of drug education to ensure the safety of those children who are going to experiment. Drug education in schools has been, and still often is, more like heavy-handed drug demonization. There is little to no practical advice, when practical advice is exactly the kind most likely to save lives. Like how, at the start of a night, you ought to test a small amount of the drugs you've bought, ideally with a testing kit. If you don't have one, always take half a pill before a whole one. Don't bomb more than 50mg of anything until you've tried putting a tiny bit up your nose.

I don't think this kind of advice is likely to inspire drug use in otherwise disinclined young people, and I do think it could avert a number of needless deaths. After testing facilities were made widely available in Switzerland, the number of deaths resulting from 'party drugs' fell to, and has remained at, zero for the past eight years. In the UK, however, MDMA-induced deaths rose from fifty-six to ninety-two in 2018, while cocaine-related fatalities doubled in the last three years. Our drug-death rates are twelve times those of Portugal, where drug use was decriminalized in 2001.

And it's clear what could help. Recently, for example, a city-wide campaign in Oslo featured photographs of people's faces with things written over them like 'Sophie did not die when she tried LSD, she'd had the substance tested and knew what it contained', 'Sarah did not die when she tried MDMA. She took just half a dose and waited to feel the effects', and 'Thomas did not die when he tried GHB. He avoided alcohol all night and dosed correctly.'

But parents, too, have a responsibility to be truthful and open minded if they want a teenager to listen to them, let alone be open with them about what's going through their mind when it comes to these things. The idea that you'll become addicted if you try drugs even once is a myth that has long been debunked because it couldn't be further from the truth. Yet it persists. The reality is, almost no one becomes addicted to drugs after taking them a few times. Even heroin. The capture rate of smoking is far higher than the capture rate of heroin, meaning that a person who tries a few cigarettes is more likely to become a smoker than a person who tries heroin a few times is to become a heroin addict. You don't become physically dependent on something until you've been taking it constantly over a long period of time, which takes a lot of commitment and money – neither of which most teenagers have. Of course, the mind can become dependent on something long before the body does, but when people say a drug's 'addictive' what they generally mean is that it's nice and people want to do it again, either to relive the high or avoid the comedown. They mean it releases some happy chemicals in your head, which makes you feel good and makes you want to repeat the experience. Getting a text also causes your brain to release happy chemicals, as does playing *Candy Crush*, masturbating, crying or eating entire sleeves of Jammie Dodgers.

In the famous Rat Park experiments of the seventies, the addictive potential of drugs was proven by putting rats alone in cages with two bottles of water: one containing heroin or cocaine water and the other containing normal, boring water. The rats would always choose the drug water, which they'd laze around sucking until they died, and apparently this proved that drugs are impossibly addictive and destructive.

But those rats were always alone and kept in shitty cages with nothing to do. When the experiments were repeated, but this time with a cage full of fun rat activities and fun rat hideouts, the rodents stopped going for the drugged water pretty much altogether and started hanging out with each other instead.

This experiment was lived out with real humans during Vietnam. In the filth and frightfulness of a brutal war, vast numbers of American troops starting smoking opium. It was readily available, astoundingly pure, and tolerated by the higher ranks, who were themselves often also using. These men were taking high-strength heroin every day for years. It terrified Nixon, who believed that once the war was over, America would be struggling to cope with an influx of traumatized, drug-addicted veterans.

He needn't have worried about the drug addiction.

Almost none of the men who returned from Vietnam continued using heroin. Even though around 50 per cent would try opioids again at some point, only 6 per cent would become re-addicted, and of those 6 per cent, a majority were men who had dabbled in heroin before being sent to fight. When asked how they managed to kick their habits, the men explained that they had lives that needed getting on with and there was no time or space in them for drugs.

That isn't to belittle the very real and serious problem of addiction. While most soldiers could use for a long time then stop altogether, for others it would have only taken a few uses to have them set on a path to lifelong addiction. But this has more to do with the people taking the drugs than the drugs themselves.

This is where it gets messier when we're talking about teenagers. In their book *The Teenage Brain*, Amy Ellis Nutt and Frances E. Jensen explain how addictive behaviours seem to form more easily during adolescence and are harder to break because of neurological differences in teenage brains. Teenagers have increased neural plasticity and neuronal activity; for those of you who prefer metaphors to scientific labels, they suggest imagining a teenage brain is like a forest, and taking heroin means leaving the well-trodden path. Their brain has never gone this way before, so this new habit barges its way through the undergrowth, knocking aside branches and tearing up ferns. The next time the teenager takes heroin, they find that the path is slightly less difficult to walk down. Eventually the path becomes cleared. Their brain finds it very easy to stroll down, again and again.

In adolescents, the brain forest isn't as overgrown as it is in adults, and it is far easier to clear new routes through it. Their brains also aren't so set in well-established routes, so taking a new one is a less dramatic change. So you might not be hugely likely to get addicted to heroin after snorting a bump, but you may be more likely to than an adult who tries the same amount.

Teaching teens about how their brains are developing might be useful. Making them self-aware can't be a bad thing. If there is a history of addiction in the family or if you've spotted signs of an addictive personality in your child, having that conversation might be worthwhile. This is in the hope that if they ever try a substance that blows them away with how enjoyable it is, they stop and think: maybe I shouldn't try that again, maybe I should look at how susceptible to it I might be. This, anyway, is the reason I try not to smoke crack any more.

IV

If I were a parent, I'd be more anxious about vodka than acid or pills or any of the other less socially acceptable ways of escaping the monotony of life on our planet.

When I was fourteen, my school organized an exchange pro-gramme with a German school. In England, the Germans were largely bored and frustrated that there was nothing to do but loiter in the town square smoking matchstick-thin roll-ups and kicking each other in the shins. In Germany, my classmates and I were overjoyed. The legal age for drinking was sixteen but none of the bartenders would blink before serving us beer. We drank. And drank. We had been warned specifically not to do this by our German teacher. Do not drink with the German students, she'd said. They are much better at it than you.

And it's true, they were. While we forced down as many drinks as possible, giddy with the freedom, they nursed a couple of beers and smoked a few cigarettes. Nothing about alcohol was particularly exciting to them. It was always around, and it wasn't a huge problem. You have a few drinks, sometimes you get a bit drunk, then you go home. Drinking is legal in the streets but there is never anything even remotely resembling the post-2 a.m. carnival of piss and puke often seen in Great Britain.

True to form, by 6 p.m. I was throwing up in a bin in the middle of the town.

'Hey,' my exchange partner said. 'You cannot be sicking in the bin. This is the police station, right there.'

'Sorry,' I said.

Why aren't you sicking in the bin too? I thought.

Alcohol is the big mumbling, puking elephant in the room of our culture. It can't be a surprise that young people are starting to turn their backs on it. According to data from an NHS Digital survey, 48 per cent of fifteen-year-old students in Britain had drunk alcohol in the past week when polled in the year 2000. By 2014, this had fallen to 18 per cent. The idea that the only way to socialize, go out, unwind, see friends, and eat any meal fancier than microwave pizza is with the aid of a significant amount of alcohol was bound to change sooner or later, in the same way that smokers have been banished to the back steps of pubs. Having said that, if you dig a little deeper into the stats surrounding alcohol consumption, you'll see that young people who do drink almost invariably drink to get extremely drunk. The idea of having one or two drinks is as alien as dial-up internet and phones without cameras. This is a trend that isn't just confined to the UK. Across Europe, youth drinking is falling, while binge drinking is on the rise.

Unfortunately, I was not swept up in the trend of teetotalism. Like a reasonable number of other young people, I chose to continue the age-old tradition of stumbling drunkenly past my limits to find out where they were. Like a smaller number of young people, I struggled to shake off this habit once adulthood loomed into view.

As I write this book, I'm a few months sober after a rocky couple of years. Many friends are years and lifetimes into sobriety. Many over-forties I know are drinking more than ever, seeing nothing wrong with bottles of wine every night and weekends spent segueing directly from hungover to tipsy. If you do it in the comfort of your own home, they reason, it isn't alcohol misuse, it's unwinding after a hard day at work. Through hard work, they have earned the right to consume large quantities of the stinky juice that makes them fat, sad, and more at risk of contracting every type of cancer.

YOLO was a short-lived internet slogan attached to reckless

teenagers, but now you're more likely to hear it coming out of the mouths of their parents.

'Oh sweet and hardworking father, why must you drink so much?'

'Because, son, you only live once!'

'But father, isn't that reason to drink less? Wouldn't you like to feel the grass between your toes and the wind rushing through your hair? Wouldn't you prefer to spend your one life cancer-free and pink-livered? Wouldn't you like to feel like sunshine in the morning?'

Older people, it seems, are far less likely to see regular drinking as a problem than the young because alcohol has been such an intrinsic part of their entire lives. It's familiar, and chances are they remember a little too fondly frolicking in the woods with stolen cans of lager and plastic beakers of gin siphoned out of dusty drinks-cabinet bottles.

It's fairly common to hear parents talk about letting their teenagers drink in the house with their friends. In these cases, the parents are often more than happy to buy alcohol for their kids too. It's better than them drinking in the street! they maintain. It's better that I know where they are!

But is it really?

I find it hard to believe that it does anything other than normalize getting drunk. So drunk, in fact, that you can't be trusted to be out in the wider world. That was my instinct, anyway, and I dug around and found some information about an interesting experiment.

Caitlin Abar of Penn State University conducted a study

of three hundred teenagers, their families, and their drinking habits. She polled the kids as they grew up and left home for the chaos of college. Those whose parents had been more tolerant of drinking while they were in school went on to drink more and binge-drink far more often than those whose parents had been completely against underage drinking. This finding was backed up by further studies by other people with letters after their names.

I had thought that the Continental model of trusting young people to drink sensibly made sense, but after reading for even half an hour about the effects of alcohol on developing brains I struggle to see the need to find a place for it at all. Just because German teenagers aren't puking in bins, it doesn't mean the drink isn't irreversibly impairing cognitive development. What's the point of looking for ways in which to allow it at all? Alcohol is not a fundamental human need, and if you believe having fun, socializing, or winding down to only be possible with the help of drink, then it suggests not that beer is invaluable but that elements of your life may need re-evaluating.

People talk about drugs being addictive but we rarely want to tackle the issue of alcohol. As we all know, certain men and women have a genetic predisposition towards addiction because the rewards systems in their brains are more sensitive to certain substances. For example, alcoholics are typically found to have naturally lower levels of serotonin than non-alcoholics. Alcohol temporarily raises levels of serotonin in the brain. Ergo, alcoholics are more likely to become dependent on drink because, for them, the effects are more pronounced.

It seems incredible that people accept heavy drinking as an inevitable part of growing up when so many studies point to such blatant neurological and physiological effects. I smile wistfully to myself when I think of the tall, intelligent, handsome person I could have become, had I not smoked and drunk through my formative years.

Instead of alcohol, young people are seeking out drugs that can be taken without hangovers, that aren't as habit-forming and tolerance-building. Hallucinogens, tranquillizers, and empathogens are the main kinds of drugs that are on the rise. They are not typically moreish. They have mild after-effects rather than recognizable hangovers or comedowns. They tend not to make you aggressive, risk-taking, or out-and-out idiotic. Instead, they help induce experiences that provide insight or provide feelings of love and deep connection. Hardly surprising that a generation of kids who feel adrift and depressed have turned to drugs that can temporarily remedy these feelings. The 2015 crime survey of England and Wales showed that the use of MDMA by young adults had spiked 84 per cent over the previous two years.

There is no shortage of journalists predicting that alcohol will be phased out over the coming decades, both because of decreased popularity and tighter restrictions on its sale. It may either be replaced by a less-harmful version of itself – like scientist David Nutt's 'alcosynth'* – or with legalized marijuana, other soft

---

* A synthetic form of alcohol that's supposed to offer its fun parts – confidence, sociability etc. – without the hangovers, stupidity, addictiveness, or cancer. Currently in trials. Quite likely to be covertly sabotaged by spies sent by your favourite brand of gin.

drugs, or some different, yet-to-be-discovered but less physically, mentally and economically harmful substances.

V

The best response to finding drugs on your kids is always going to involve trying to maintain a level of calmness. Too often, while parents will turn a blind, winking eye to drinking, woe betide young Oscar if he comes home with dinner-plate eyes. . .

'Are you on drugs? I'm calling the police! You're going to rehab.'

I have seen any number of parents go apeshit because they thought that finding a baggie in their kid's pocket meant their child would now require three months of cold-turkey rehab in a converted Cotswolds monastery. Overreacting to drugs has never convinced anyone not to take them. Usually, punishing someone harshly for finding them with drugs makes them feel more alienated and upset, driving them even further towards the behaviours you wanted to control in the first place.

It might sound like Waldorf/Steiner parenting, but asking rather than accusing when it comes to drugs is always going to be more productive. What have you been taking? Are you sure it's that? Have you tested it? Do you feel okay? Was everyone else safe? Rather than driving drug use into shadows where it can't be monitored, this opens a channel of communication.

In the early hours of a summer morning in 2015, five Jersey teenagers were caught dumping their dying friend by the side of a country road. He was overdosing on drugs after a night spent partying. Rather than call for help, they'd chosen to try and get him as far from possible from the house to avoid being prosecuted by police for giving him drugs. He died. They were all sentenced to years in prison for manslaughter.

Similar incidents have happened again and again.

Young people hesitate to call the police when friends fall ill through drugs, because they know there's a chance they could be prosecuted for dealing or manslaughter, even if their only crime was buying three pills and giving out two to friends.

For every drug death in Britain there is usually a group of friends left behind who have to cope both with the loss of someone they cared about, while also being investigated like criminals by the police. What's so terrible about it is how avoidable some of these deaths could be if the law wasn't so determined to lock up sixteen-year-olds who have very clearly not been trying to hurt anyone or make money from selling drugs. These are kids celebrating the end of exams and the beginning summer holidays, not vicious drug dealers forcing their wares on unsuspecting children.

An easy way to make sure that young people aren't afraid to seek medical help when they need it is to help them make sure they won't be put in jail for having shared pills with their friends. Until the law changes, it wouldn't hurt to have prearranged lies. If I were a parent, I'd advise my kids that if someone is in trouble and they need medical attention, they have everyone involved agree to state that the drugs came from a bush, the internet, or a strangely generous man in the park. Anything will do, as long as it's agreed upon by the group, and doesn't implicate one individual. Yes, this book is suggesting that your children lie to the police, but only because it might one day mean the difference between life and death.

Staying calm in the face of narcotics doesn't mean you should share your drugs with your kids. When I talked to Simon and Samson, two boys from London, about how they got their drugs, something very surprising came up: 'Sometimes someone's parents give them to us so they know what we're taking,' said Simon. This was a frightening and alien idea to me. If my mum had ever tried to give me drugs, I would have started googling how to get her sectioned. But these were kids at otherwise normal schools with otherwise normal parents.

'How do the parents get the drugs?' I wanted to know.

'Well, they take them too, like at festivals or whatever. I guess they have dealers.'

This came as a shock. Maybe, I thought, it's some kind of way of rendering substances uncool – I can't help thinking it might make drugs significantly less exciting if your parents both take them and offer them to you. (To be clear, I'm not talking about particularly addictive drugs, but drugs that are generally taken in order to have a one-off experience, such as mushrooms, ketamine, or MDMA. Even I can recognize that if your parents are drug addicts, you're more likely to fall into addiction yourself.)

When I mentioned this to teenagers outside of London and certain major cities, they were as shocked as I was. There was always someone with a 'weed mum' who invariably didn't have a job, only went out with awful men, and would happily share a joint with you, but no one's parents would dream of giving them powder drugs.

'So, the parents are junkies?'

'You don't really get MDMA junkies.'

'Why would you give your kids drugs though?'

'So you can be sure what's in it.'

'But. . .'

I heard stories of drugs being found in bedrooms and returned to teenagers, as well as homes – the homes of otherwise normal parents – being suggested as the place where drugs are taken, again, 'rather than you doing it on the street'. This, however, remains an unusual way of doing things for most people, and tends to spring from parents who are nostalgic for their own drug-using past (or present, as the case may be). 'She would kill me if she found any drugs,' was something I heard more than once. 'Dad would throw me out of the house.' And this is important, because young people often cite losing the respect or trust of their parents as one of the key factors in deciding not to take drugs. But again, a balance needs to be struck between your kids not wanting to take drugs out of respect and not wanting to seek help out of fear. It is through maintaining this connection, through having this level of trust, that the most dangerous behaviours can be avoided.

More than anything, you need to be able to listen and kids need to feel free to speak. Perhaps the best thing for a group of teenagers is knowing a parent who you're sure won't freak out if things have got out of hand. When I was growing up, there was always one person's parent we knew we could go to if things went to shit. If there hadn't been, I'm sure certain incidents would have ended far more disastrously than they did. There are more varieties of drugs than ever and they are all more readily accessible than they've ever been, which means there are also far more ways for things to go wrong.

It might be hard trying to act calmly when your heart is screaming: You stupid prick! What do you think you're doing! You could be dead! It also might mean that, if something ever goes wrong, you'll be the first rather than the last to know. Instead of rolling his body along the hard shoulder of a motorway, Oscar's team of panicked friends might call to let you know he's in trouble, and you might be able to help.

Don't forget:

- Letting kids drink in the house does nothing but increase the likelihood of them drinking more than they should later on. It might feel reassuring in the short term but may well be damaging in the long run.
- Building a reputation as someone who can be trusted is invaluable. Burying your head in the sand and insisting your child is too angelic ever to try anything stronger than half a pint of shandy might just mean they never confide in you for fear of tarnishing that image and disappointing you.
- Just because you're unfamiliar with something doesn't mean it's dangerous. Taking a reasonable-sized dose of MDMA is safer than drinking four litres of super-strength cider, and punishing one but not the other is only going to engender resentment.

Homework:

Order a gram of MDMA from the Silk Road 4.0 and try wrapping a third of it in a blue Rizla and swallowing it.

Just kidding.

Download the Tor browser, find the address for a drug marketplace, and have a look around. It's fun, sort of like going to the London Dungeon or watching *Poltergeist* with the lights off.

Lesson Seven:

Kids Watch Porn

First times, golden showers, and getting it wrong

I

At the age of thirteen I arranged to lose my virginity to a girl under her parents' living-room table. She was a few years older than me, had dyed-black hair, and spent a lot of time uploading terribly recorded covers of Tegan and Sara songs to the internet. After a handful of nocturnal online conversations, we'd begun a relationship that consisted mostly of exchanging bathroom selfies and heavily breathing into phones.

She was terrified of talking on the phone but felt comfortable enough to be frank when it came to what a vicar might call 'heavy petting'. Touch this, she'd say. Not that, this. It was intimidating, illuminating, and helped us to avert several catastrophes caused by the overenthusiastic fingering of an under-experienced boy.

Anyway, under the living-room table seemed the safest place

for our first time. Upstairs, her parents and sister were sleeping. The lights were off. A muted TV cast shadows across the carpet.

'Are you sure you want to do this?' I asked.

'Yes, are you?'

We put down a towel. We pulled our underwear down to just above knee level. We fumbled with a needlessly pineapple-flavoured condom. I remember feeling alarmed by how long it was. They're like guitar strings, I reasoned, putting it on. They just stretch far longer than is necessary.

'Did you pinch the end shut?' she whispered.

'Why would I pinch the end shut?'

'Not the end of your dick – of the condom.'

'Which end?'

'Take it off. We'll have to put another one on now.'

Luckily, because she was older, she had spent more time in sex education. And she'd listened too, whereas I was usually focused on phone games and getting through a bag of chocolate chips labelled by Tesco as an ingredient rather than a mid-morning snack. The only real research I'd done in the lead-up to our first time was upping my porn intake from roughly fifteen to forty-five minutes a day. There was almost no category that I was unwilling to explore. Every age group, ethnicity, size, shape, and configuration seemed to offer something new. I had seen fifteen men queue up to cum on the face of a woman dressed like Little Red Riding Hood. I had seen an elderly man spanking an eighteen-year-old

---

* I don't mind admitting that, at thirteen, I may not have been one hundred per cent certain that a vagina could not taste things.

girl in a pine forest. A boy called Richard had even sent over mp4s of a woman having sex with a Labrador. Watch this, he'd said. It's sick.

'Is it okay?' I asked.

'It's fine.'

I took her right breast in my fingers and pulled, like an octopus trying to peel a piece of freshly dropped gum off the pavement. I let go. I pulled. I let go. I pulled.

'Why are you grabbing my boob like that?' she whispered. 'It hurts.'

Meekly, I told her I didn't know, and stopped. I did know. I had seen this kind of boob-grabbing in porn and assumed there was something titillating (sorry) about it for women. I thought, perhaps not unreasonably, that this was a kind of special move that might bring a woman to climax.

As mistaken ideas learned from porn go, overenthusiastic boob-yanking is fairly innocuous. If you were an alien who had only ever watched porn, you could be forgiven for thinking that human sex follows a fairly regimented pattern:

- The male human receives a rabid, wide-eyed blowjob from the female human, who is kneeling down. Sometimes she will try and get the penis out of her mouth so she can breathe. If she tries this, the male human will seize hold of her conveniently long hair and prevent her from doing so.
- Parting the female human's legs, the male human will enter her and begin a style of sex considered so boring it is known as 'missionary'.

- The male human will flip the female human over and continue penetration from behind, in a style of sex considered so animal it is known as 'doggy'.
- Painlessly, the man will transition from having sex with the female human's vagina to having sex with her anus. The transition will have been the female human's idea and will have been signalled by her saying something like 'now stick it in my ass'.
- The male human will withdraw his penis and gruntingly ejaculate all over the female human's grateful face.

Let's imagine our hypothetical David Bowie starman falls to earth and is ready to get down to business. He has just spent the previous three years hurtling through the universe in a spaceship, jacking off to *Girls Gone Apeshit 4* and fantasizing about one day relieving Flavio of his role.

'I'm going to have sex,' he's been thinking, on loop. 'I'm going to have sex so much.'

This alien, then, presuming he owned a penis, would perhaps feel entitled to a blowjob as soon as he had found a consenting human partner. He would feel fine with taking hold of the woman's long hair and bouncing it off his straggly blue mass of pubes. Tears running down the woman's cheeks would not be unprecedented. Neither would gagging.

Following this, our alien friend might arrange the woman in various positions and pound away, perhaps feeling confused if she doesn't respond with tennis player sounds to his frantic pumping. To clarify, he may ask rhetorical questions such as 'do you like that?' in a voice much deeper than his normal talking voice. He may also say other things, things involving sluts or daddies or any of the other ten million fetishes that have spawned ten hundred million even more obscure fetishes in the far reaches of the internet.

Tired of the boring old vagina, he might then hotfoot it to the nearest bumhole. And she loves it! She cannot get enough of his dick in her ass! Your dick is deep in my ass, she might mutter, if she's bothered to learn her lines.

But fear not, this is not how it ends. He will always remember to whip it out in time to discharge his alien gunk onto the woman's face.

Hopefully, if the girl has also seen porn, she will know to gleefully lick the semen off her lips. She will not feel comfortable, nor will she feel surprised. After all, the face is where men are supposed to cum.* We're not aiming for babies here.

Did I do it right, he will wonder.

Did I do it right, she will wonder.

After finishing under the living-room table, my girlfriend and I stood up to find that the towel was dotted with blood. My girlfriend was distraught. Do we put it in the bin? Burn it? Pour bleach over it? In the end, she woke up her mum, who gave her a cuddle, threw away the towel and gently suggested we wait until everyone was out of the house next time. This was not the way my own mother reacted when, ten minutes

---

* I once had sex with a girl before which we'd agreed to use the famously reliable withdrawal method of contraception. After I pulled out and ejaculated on her belly, she said, sincerely, 'Thanks for not cumming on my face.' I find it difficult to believe that porn isn't having some sort of effect on the kids.

into an argument concerning facial piercings, I revealed myself to be sexually active.

'And I love it!' I announced, not actually sure if I did.

Strangely enough, some years after that night, I would be asked by a woman to grab her boob, then grab it harder, then grab it so hard it felt as though it would come off in my hand. I am consistently amazed by the diversity on show throughout our species.

II

Fairly recently, a seven-pints-in friend I used to be at school with divulged the reason a girl named Steph had broken up with him back in sixth form. Their break-up had not seemed particularly interesting or dramatic at the time (my main concerns back then were sourcing vodka, codeine, Swiss Rolls and notes from mum that said I had tonsillitis). He had been going out with a girl and then he was no longer going out with the girl – that was all I really remembered.

Back in the future, we were playing I've Never in a bar with flypaper floor. For anyone who's never played, this involves taking it in turns to say something like, 'I have never eaten a lobster', and then everyone who has eaten a lobster glugs from their drink, signalling their guilt. The inevitable questions came up: threesomes, gay experiences, shitting yourself, stealing, lying, crying, masturbating in places you're not supposed to masturbate in.

'I have never done a golden shower,' came next.

The friend downed his lager.

'Yeah, right,' said someone.

'Course you have,' said someone else. 'With who?'

He muttered Steph's name. No one believed him. Half an hour later, we went outside to smoke a cigarette and he told me the full story. He'd been suggesting she piss on him for a few weeks when they finally found themselves alone and, getting drunk on plundered drinks-cabinet vodka in her parents' house, she relented. They undressed in the bathroom and she pissed on his chest and dick in the shower.

'Why did you want to do that?' I asked.

'I don't know,' he said. 'I've seen it. I thought it would be hot.'

'Was it?'

'No, it was horrible and itchy. And she cried.'

'She cried?'

'It wasn't like she didn't want to do it. Just when she started she got embarrassed and weird.'

In short, she pissed on him in the shower, neither of them enjoyed it, and she broke up with him the week after that. He says she never offered a concrete reason.

It reminded me of another break-up at school, involving a friend named Luke.

Luke came bouncing into the classroom one day and joyously recounted weekend adventures with a girl from school he'd been going out with for a couple of months. It did not, at the age of sixteen, seem remotely possible to anyone that he had 'bent her over and fucked her in the ass', let alone that he had done this in front of an open window in her parents' house while said parents were downstairs watching *Coronation Street*. From the girl's perspective, it was also not a heart-warming story to hear circulating about yourself.

Later, someone saw him sobbing in the passenger seat of her metallic Peugeot 206. She was yelling at him to get out of the car. He was, presumably, swearing undying love.

'Yeah, I sacked her off,' Luke later told everyone, pockets bulging with used tissues. 'She didn't want to try a threesome.'

It would not be the first or the last time someone regurgitated the plot of a porno as though it was a recent episode from their life. What could be cooler than doing porn things! I mean, having a girlfriend, probably, and friends who didn't think you were a terrible person.

One of the biggest impacts of watching a lot of porn when you're young is that, rather than participating in sex, you can end up performing it. And the performance of it becomes the goal, rather than any kind of mutual pleasure. All that matters is that you want to do sex right, following the preapproved order and script.

Say, for example, you start watching porn at eleven. It shapes your understanding of how long and hard sex 'ought' to be. When you hit fifteen and find that your stamina doesn't measure up to Ben Dover and Ruby Crystal's, you panic. But it's okay. This is 2020. Mum takes varenicline to keep her off cigarettes, dad takes minoxidil to coax his hair back, and the dog's on SSRIs because we're all convinced it's depressed.

Whatever's wrong, there's a pill for it. It's hardly surprising that a recent trend has seen increasingly younger people turn to Viagra. Fifteen-year-old boys are taking blue pills to give them marathon boners. And it's so easy. With a PayPal account they can order Viagra and have it delivered by tomorrow. This will equip them to have sex the way sex is supposed to be had. Thank God for the internet, always on hand to offer solutions to the problems it has created.

Nobody has made it clear to our young studs that it's unlikely any girl their age will enjoy enduring an hour and a half of confused sex because her self-conscious boyfriend has swallowed a handful of internet Viagra.

Possibly the scariest and most inescapable thing about porn is that there's no going back. It isn't like smoking or drinking, where warning labels can be slapped on and prices hiked up, dissuading new users and making old ones think twice. It is free and constantly available, in forms ranging from virtual reality to nudes swapped between phones.

If you're fourteen and you hear about porn, you'll at least be curious, and your curiosity will not require you to do anything but stick your hand in your pocket and pull out your phone.

Naked ladies may be the first search.

A2M CFNM* may be the tenth.

The sheer breadth of available material will spur on a kind of frenzied search for newer, stranger, more exciting things. Eventually one kind of scenario will become boring, and you'll go in search of something else. No one ever tastes vanilla ice cream once and sticks with that flavour for eternity. You discover the rest of the Neapolitan rainbow, followed by increasingly complex

---

* For those who are not porn connoisseurs, this would be ass to mouth porn, featuring a clothed female and a naked male.

variations on chocolate, bad imitations of exotic fruits, and bizarre savoury concoctions studded with nuts and flakes.

If you don't believe me, here are the top twelve searches made from the United Kingdom on Pornhub during 2018:

1. Lesbian
2. Milf
3. Massage
4. Big Tits
5. Squirt
6. Public
7. Step Mom
8. Lesbians scissoring
9. Asian
10. Creampie
11. JOI*
12. British chav†

That's all very well, you might think, but my little angel certainly isn't jerking off to chavvy Asian stepmoms baking creampies‡ with their big-breasted wives. Other statistics, however, also kindly provided by Pornhub, tell us that most porn is viewed after 10

---

* Again, for those who are unfamiliar, this stands for 'jerk off instruction', which generally involves a woman repeatedly telling the viewer to masturbate for her.
† Although 'chav' has all but left the British lexicon over the past few years, porn users seem a little slow on the uptake.
‡ A creampie is when the man ejaculates into the woman's vagina and sort of simultaneously pulls out so that you can see his cum dribble out of her. I doubt you bake them.

p.m., with the notable exception of a significant peak around 4 p.m., or the time that everyone's getting home from school. What's the likely effect of such a variety of porn on schoolkids? It doesn't seem a stretch to imagine that when you're used to trawling through endless thumbnails of different women each night, committing sexually to one person in real life might become difficult.

No, but really, you might insist, my son doesn't watch porn, nor does my dad, or my boyfriend, or any of the other kind-hearted, Jesus-loving men I know.

Except they almost definitely do.

In 2009, the University of Montreal attempted to conduct a study that compared the views of men who watched porn with the views of those who didn't. The study could not go ahead: they couldn't find any men who didn't watch porn. They also discovered that the average age at which men first watched porn was ten.

It seems terrifying. It might be, it might not be.

There are studies that claim watching porn can make men treat women more callously, make them less empathetic and take rape less seriously. There are other studies that claim watching porn has absolutely no effect on behaviour and can actually contribute to a decrease in sexual crime by offering an outlet for certain sexual fantasies.

You can find evidence to back up whatever it is you want to believe. Ultimately, porn seems to affect different people in different ways. We know now that video games are unlikely to cause young people to act more violently, and it's likely that most fears around porn are similarly exaggerated. The danger comes when people learn sex exclusively from porn, when they have no other idea of what loving sex is or can be. It would be like learning how to drive from watching monster truck rallies or learning how to date by watching *Take Me Out*.

What is clear is that porn is changing the way young people perceive sex. Acts that would have been considered deviant twenty years ago are now normal and even expected. The question is whether or not this marks some kind of genuine sexual liberation or just a different standard that people feel obliged to conform to, without regard for what it is they actually want.

III

As mentioned earlier, the year of our Lord 2014 was the year in which over five hundred naked pictures of celebrities were stolen from personal phones and plastered across various corners of the internet.

'Why take naked photos of yourself in the first place!' crowed my thoroughly disapproving Aunt Alice.

Jennifer Lawrence stepped up to explain. 'I was in a loving, healthy relationship for four years,' she said. 'If your man's not looking at you, he's looking at porn.'

Something immediately sounds off with this idea. You might, reasonably, suggest:

It's not your responsibility to make anyone cum whenever their genitals start humming.

And:

In an age of ubiquitous video, it might do you some good to shut your eyes and try to imagine something for a change. Resigning yourself to having a boyfriend that is completely helpless to do anything other than jerk off to photos of naked women seems a little sad. Surely we can ask slightly more of men than that?

You can argue about whether or not it's ever okay for young people to send each other naked pictures of themselves, but ultimately, it doesn't matter. You might as well disapprove of earthquakes or sneezing. Parents and teachers are no longer the gatekeepers of this kind of behaviour, because these behaviours are entirely new, and almost entirely unpoliceable.

For about a week in Year 9, everyone at school possessed a video of a girl from a neighbouring school masturbating on webcam. This wasn't ordinary masturbation. While being encouraged by a boy from our school, the girl went from using a vibrator to using the grip end of a hockey stick, by way of a banana, a cola bottle, and a tube of hair clay.

'Have you seen it yet?' people whispered in corridors.

'No, can you send it?'

The video somehow reached the police. An effort was made to retrace the steps the video had taken. Several boys were pulled out of classrooms and interrogated by police officers. Where had they got the footage from, the officers would ask, at which point the boys would point fingers at other boys, who would then be hoisted out of more classrooms and made to point fingers at more boys.

Ultimately, no one was punished.

Whether or not we should have the freedom to send each other pictures of our genitals in private is a moot point, because it's impossible to ensure they remain private. Again, this is the most important thing to communicate to teens about their actions in the modern world: nothing ever goes away. Unless you pat someone down for technology, lead them into a room in which a naked picture of you is hanging, then lead them out again, there will always be a possibility that they could show this photo to someone, a friend could stumble across it, or it could be stolen in a hack. At which point, the picture belongs to the world forever.

No fifteen-year-old has ever responded to 'Can I see a pic?' by saying 'The *Guardian* says our developing brains are unable to responsibly make decisions about how we share images of ourselves at a time when doing so could have unforeseen, long-term consequences.'

When you're young and tending to a boner, there can very easily be no thought of the future. So here are a few tips, which you could pass on to your teen in your own style. They are not from me, by the way. I have never sent a naked photo. I don't like my body enough and don't trust anyone else. Instead I asked someone who had sent me a number of pictures in the past which rules she adhered to every time:

- Never put your face in the shot. That's stupid. Anyway, they don't care about the face.
- If you have tattoos, hide your fucking tattoos. Same with

freckles and third nipples and whatever. Nothing that's identifiable.

- If you're sending this, you have to get something back. Don't let them sponge off you.
- If you're a guy, don't send dick pics to people you don't know. Or to people you do know but aren't sexting with. Just don't send dick pics, unless specifically asked.

With the internet, an entirely new set of behaviours have emerged to be reckoned with. This is dangerous territory to be caught in. Victims might miss out on justice, offenders might be punished too harshly, too leniently, or not at all. All we can do is try to be considerate, both to the people around us, and our future selves.

IV

So what do we do? As we saw before, it doesn't matter how many restrictions are imposed upon it, porn is not going to disappear from the lives of teenagers. The real way to bring about change is to counteract the fantasy of it with some more realistic expectations. You have to find a way of making sure young people are aware of just how little they should take away from what they're seeing, and how it's far more likely that enjoyable sex will result from consideration and thoughtfulness than from trying to emulate porn.

Good luck to any of you who decide to attempt this with

sit-down talks and diagrams. If my mum ever tried to speak to me about asking before anal, I would have jumped through a window. There would not be enough cable ties on earth to hold me in place if she had ever started lecturing on the ethics of fingering. However, I had no qualms ransacking her bedroom in search of *The Joy of Sex: The Ultimate Revised Edition* and *The Kama Sutra*, which seems to be a common method amongst people of a certain age. As with most things, the best tactic is to make information available without forcing it on anyone.

As ever, school and the role it can play in guiding teenagers is a different matter. School seems the ideal place to try and teach certain things because the students cannot run away. You aren't allowed to escape from a classroom, no matter how uncomfortable you might feel.

A more wide-ranging, open style of sex education, done with someone who is specially trained in it would, in my opinion, be ideal. It still feels like the majority of schools rely on the spare hours of reluctant biology teachers. As a result, most boys could point out fallopian tubes on a diagram but will guess that a vulva is a type of hat.

Though it might prove agony for the teacher, opening any kind of dialogue on the subject is always going to be preferable to nothing. The goal is not necessarily to turn teenagers into Casanovas but to get them at least thinking about the issues surrounding sex. Here's how it might work:

Teacher: Today, in sex education, we will be learning about sex and how to do it.

Student: But, miss, we did sex last week. The penis enters the vagina and unleashes semen into it.

Teacher: Over the coming weeks, we'll be covering the practicalities. Today this will mean foreplay, otherwise known as heavy petting. This can be a standalone activity and it can be a prelude to the beast with two backs.

Student: Miss, what's the beast with two backs?

Teacher: What do you think it is, Rogers?

Student: Is it a Siamese cat?

Teacher: We don't say Siamese any more, Rogers, it's racist. We say conjoined. And no. It alludes to the deed itself. Now, given that you are a class of boys, we'll first need to cover digital stimulation. It is not the aim of this to get as deep into the vagina as possible as quickly as possible and root around as though you are searching for change down the back of a sofa.

Student: But, miss, what if that's how they like it?

Teacher: How do you know 'how they like it', Singh?

Student: Just do, miss.

Teacher: Have you ever asked someone how they like it?

Student: No, miss.

Teacher: I suggest you practise. It isn't difficult. 'How is that? Should I continue?' Unless you've been endowed with telepathic abilities, which, judging by your mock results I doubt, it will never hurt to ask what a person wants and what feels best. How would you feel if I inserted a whisk into your anus without any warning?

Student: Miss, that's gross.

Teacher: Well, aren't you glad I asked first?

Student: I would never put a whisk in someone, miss.

Teacher: Oh, a round of applause for Jenkins, everyone. The last remaining gentleman. Now, who wants to come up here and find the clitoris on this model for me?

Student: I'll do it, miss.

Teacher: Up you come.

Student: Is that it?

Teacher: That's my pencil sharpener, Pearson.

Student: What about that?

Teacher: That is your own finger.

Student: Is it this?

Teacher: Please sit down, Pearson, and leave my purse on my chair where it belongs. The clitoris is this hood here, at the top of the vagina.

Student: Boyz in da hood!

Teacher: Get out, Dixon, go and sit outside Mrs Clark's office, and repeat your little joke for her benefit. Now, many women will not orgasm from penetrative sex, but need stimulation of the glans clitoris, the external part of the clitoris, here, to be added to the equation... The clitoral hood can be gently opened up like this, which will also often lead to the vagina growing wet, allowing a penis, or whatever else is involved, to more easily enter. Some women may not self-lubricate and might need additional help.

Student: Like, spit on it?

Teacher: Again, Rogers, that's something you might want to discuss with your partner. Personally, if you tried to spit on any part of me, it would be the last time you had teeth to spit through. Every step should be consensual, and no one should feel uncomfortable at any moment. You know how you don't have any qualms about demanding your mothers make you tea? This is how your partner should feel.

Student: But sometimes they say no and you have to keep asking, miss.

Teacher: Do you really, Richards?

Student: Yes.

Teacher: No, you don't.

Student: But in a film, they say no first, and you have to prove you want them.

Teacher: And this is a trope in books and TV that have caused billions of women feeling threatened and pressured for hundreds of years. Take no for an answer. Use your heads. Be human beings. Sex is not the same as pestering someone to go to the cinema with you, it is an intimate act which can have emotional repercussions that ripple through a person's entire life. Never put a desire to unload your testicles above another person's right to live undisturbed. Go and masturbate in a locked toilet if you have to. Just treat other people with kindness and respect. It may feel as though your tiny dicks are the centre of the universe, but they are not.

This, I think, is the kind of teacher Sam, Steph, and I would all have benefited from.

Don't forget:

- It is inevitable that teenagers will watch porn. It is not inevitable that they believe it resembles real sex.
- You probably don't want to sit down and try to tell your child that they ought not to try fisting. Your kid doesn't want that either. But there are TV shows and documentaries that stumble through the awkward conversations so you don't have to. They might be uncomfortable to watch, but not as uncomfortable as the sex that can result from trying to emulate porn.
- A 2019 study by David Wood et al. found that people who viewed porn were more likely to dehumanize others and act unethically, while the famous 2005 study by Ariely and Loewenstein found that men in a state of arousal were five times more likely to consider drugging a woman in order to have sex with her. This is why ideas of consent and respect must be drilled into boys at every opportunity.

Homework:

As a society, we act like it's a big mystery that socks always disappear and we end up with bags filled with odd ones. It's not a mystery. I know where the socks go. The socks go on the end of teenage dicks and get jerked off into, because they are so convenient for it you'd be forgiven for thinking that wearing them on your feet wasn't just a bonus use discovered after they'd been invented to soak up semen. If you have a son, try finding his crusty sock and replacing it with a roll of kitchen towel. This may save you money in the long run.

That, however, is a long-term project. In the short term, try watching some porn. It doesn't have to be radical and you don't have to watch a full forty minutes. But even having a scroll through what's on offer can prove enlightening. Try xHamster or Pornhub.

Interlude 3:

Sleep for the Reluctant

Virtually no one is getting enough sleep. You know that and I know that, yet very few of us bother to try and change things. In the course of writing this book, I have not spoken to a single person who is getting the amount of sleep they are supposed to. Not a single adult, nor a single adolescent. Scientists say that teenagers should be getting more sleep than both their parents and their younger siblings, yet they frequently get far less than either of those groups. The average seems to be between six and seven hours, with many getting under five and a half, compared to the recommended amount of nine hours. Getting more sleep is like eating five fruit and veg a day or not drinking more than five beers a week: we know what we're supposed to do, yet we don't do it.

At school, almost everyone I knew was perpetually tired. Kids clutched jumbo coffee cups, munched Dextro energy squares, and downed those cold, sugary cappuccinos perched beside Innocent smoothies in the ready-to-eat section of Tesco. We drank towering silver bottles of off-brand energy drink. Handfuls of caffeine tablets disappeared into our yawning mouths. One boy in our form drank two litres of Kick every day until his heart started stuttering and a doctor told him he had to quit. 'I'm trying to cut down,' he'd mournfully tell whoever asked. And smoking, as well as vaping, became common crutches for the chronically tired.

I coped with not wanting to wake up by not waking up. Or by waking up, putting on school clothes, waiting for my parents to leave, and then going back to sleep. Or by smoking a lot of cigarettes and drinking a variety of coffee that came in a bright jar with a warning label on it. Or by simply falling asleep face down on my desk like I'd been shot through the back of the head.

A lack of sleep impacts on almost every area of life. It might be the most dangerous thing we still refuse to take seriously and it can be especially dangerous for teenagers, who aren't always making the sanest decisions at the best of times, let alone after months of exhaustion. As a parent, one of the best things you can do is make sure your teenager gets plenty of sleep.

There are two main reasons why this generation isn't getting enough sleep. One is easily fixable, and one would require significant societal reshuffling.

1. Screens

Our bodies only know to power-down for the day when our brains release melatonin. 'All right,' the melatonin tells your cells, 'time for everyone to bed down and get some rest.' The only clock melatonin has to judge bedtime by is light. It sits behind the eyeballs, waiting for the sun to go down so that it can charge around getting everyone prepared for the dream world.

But how does it tell the sun has gone down when we're sitting under bright lights staring into other bright lights? And blue light, the kind produced by phones and computers, has a short wavelength and is by far the best at telling melatonin it isn't yet needed.

So melatonin is released later than it should be, people fall asleep later, and they also have less REM sleep, which doctors are increasingly deciding might be the most restorative chapter of sleep.

Aside from the physiological effects of blue light on your body, phones and computers are also just plain distracting. Why would your teenager want to lie quietly in the dark trying to convince their head to switch itself off when they can watch endless videos of pop stars tripping over while smugly prancing about on stage. The world in their phone never sleeps, so why should they?

2. Schedules

Teenagers are not supposed to wake up at seven o'clock. They're not just being lazy pricks by refusing to get out of bed – their bodies aren't yet ready to start the day. During puberty, the body's circadian rhythm shifts forward a few hours, meaning adolescents won't really feel ready for bed until around midnight. The bodies of teenagers want to go to sleep late and wake later, but we've rigged things up in such a way that they're never allowed to do this.

We know this delayed sleep theory is true, not just because studies have shown it, but because schools that have implemented later start times continually find themselves playing host to happier, healthier, more alert and ready-to-learn kids. The only reason I can see for all educational establishments not having changed things by now is because half of their kids are dropped off at school by parents on the way to work, so it's inconvenient if they need to be in a couple of hours later than Barbara needs to be at the bank. Still, waking a famously unenthusiastic group of people up before they're ready on a daily basis for the most biologically confusing years of their lives seems unhelpful. It might be easier for mum and dad, but at what cost?

On days when I *really* struggled to emerge from my duvet cocoon, I was given the wet flannel. 'Get your lazy ass out of bed!' came the rallying cry. It was often said that I failed to reach my full potential. If I had to point fingers, I would point at least a couple at my damp mattress.

Sleep affects every cell in the human body. It is terrifyingly important. It is so important that when I first read about how important it was, I became so stressed that I couldn't sleep.

Lack of sleep is connected most obviously to irritability, mood instability, and poor decision making. These are all things that are already present in teenagers, and adding to them is never going to make life easier for anyone. But not getting enough sleep is also tied to a host of other, more serious problems. Studies have linked sleep deprivation to obesity, weakened immune systems, digestive issues, depression, anxiety, cancer, high blood pressure, lack of self-control, and fatal accidents. Aside from these, sleep is particularly necessary to adolescents because it is the time at which their brains work on restructuring themselves, turning your beloved Oscar from a lively angel into a scruffy and sluggish young bogeyman.

Chronic sleep deprivation can also lead to young people being misdiagnosed as suffering from ADHD or depression, when in fact it's the lack of quality rest that's preventing them from functioning properly. Inability to focus or low mood may simply be down to not getting enough shut-eye. Altering sleep patterns for teenagers can be three times as effective at alleviating depression as medication. It's such a huge finding that you'd be forgiven for wondering whether the statistics about mental health might be slightly different if teenagers were having their glowing devices taken off them.

The habits formed in adolescence can, if left unchecked, become some of the most difficult to change; as our resident neuroscientists explained, you cut paths through the jungle and spend the rest of your life walking them. I fell asleep every night with Radio 4 playing from a bright, old blue-light emitting hi-fi. In the years since, I've probably only fallen asleep a handful of times without a soothing, Oxbridge professor rambling in my ear.

Until schools do what's best for their students and let them have a lie-in, there are a few changes that can help.

- If the option ever comes up, choose the school closer to home. It seems like a special kind of hell, rousing kids when they don't want to get up and sending them on a long journey to a place they don't want to be. Some kids at my school had hour-and-a-half-long journeys in, and you could tell. They'd always be the most pallid, sluggish, and likely to snore during physics. They'd be off sick far more than anyone else. They'd be more likely to slap you if you inadvertently trod on their toes or took their seat. I think any benefit gleaned from going to a 'better', further-away school will almost always be cancelled out by the inevitable chronic sleep deprivation caused by rolling Oscar out of bed at six every morning.

- If he absolutely has to get up at six, Oscar probably shouldn't have a phone under his pillow. A 2016 study of almost three thousand students found that some were waking up ten times a night to check their phones. Many received nearly one hundred notifications over the course of a night. Three quarters reported that they knew full well phone use in the witching hour made them less able to focus on work during the day, and they still couldn't resist. So get Oscar an alarm clock instead of having him use the phone, maybe one of those ones that gradually brightens like a sunrise.

- Basic 'sleep hygiene' also helps. It's stuff we all know and really just means no blue light two hours before bed, absolute darkness in the bedroom, no caffeine after four, and never using the bed for anything other than sleep and auto-erotic asphyxiation. One of the easiest tricks is to reduce the amount of blue light your phone is giving off. Most smartphones can do this. There will be a setting, somewhere. It's called 'night shift' on the iPhone and the only change you'll notice is a slightly warmer-coloured display. There are also specialist sunglasses that can filter out the blue light from laptops.

- The new generation of young people respond best to facts. If you present them with studies proving that life will be shittier if they aren't sleeping, they'll be more amenable than if you order them into bed early.

- It might feel like a long shot, but trying to make sleep more exciting through something like a dream diary could work too. There are apps for this, but embedding phones even more deeply into a part of life that they generally fuck up might not be the way to go. The most potent sedative I had as a teenager was a trashy paperback dream encyclopaedia. It talked about discoveries that had come about through dreams, and how you could go on adventures of your own choosing via lucid dreaming. Night after night, I fell asleep trying to will myself into controllable, Hogwarts-centred dreams.

- Let them sleep in at the weekends. Don't force them to wake up early for church, chores, car-boot sales, or family outings to urban farms. There is a reason teenagers want to hibernate on Saturdays – they've just spent five days waking up before their bodies are ready to.

Anything you can do to help your kids get more sleep will go a long way. Remember, Donald Trump beds down for only three or four hours a night. Margaret Thatcher slept for three to four. Silvio Berlusconi is currently getting two or three.

You should make sure your kids get enough sleep.

Lesson Eight:

Everything's an Advert

Self-perception, acne, and photo-editing

I

For teenagers, the body is often the biggest source of pain and confusion, the main focus of time and attention, and a gallery space for exhibitions of rebellion. A few whiteheads on the forehead can signal the end of the world, while half a shaved head will let Mum know exactly what you think of her admonitions to avoid pissing on the toilet seat. You will keep a mental diary of pube growth. Your genitals will never be the right size or shape.

You probably remember your teenage years as the time when you felt most ill at ease in your body. As you grow older, you want to kick your younger self in the shins for not appreciating what you had at the time. You were so thin, so smooth, and so silky-haired! But all you felt back then was gawky and self-conscious.

And young people today report feeling more self-conscious than ever.* You don't have to look much further than the internet to try and work out why. Twenty years ago, how many photos would a teenager have had taken of them? Possibly holiday photos, possibly birthday photos, and possibly yearly school snaps taken against lurid mauve backgrounds. Now teens are photographing themselves all of the time. Or if they're not, they're constantly looking at pictures of other people, both of which make them feel their imperfections ever more acutely. They'll see more faces and bodies through their phone than they ever will in real life, and the real faces will pale in comparison to the phone faces. The difference between now and the pre-social media era is the blurring of the line that separates reality from fantasy.

When film stars were seen only in films, they were viewed almost as belonging to a different species. Of course I don't look like them, you'd think, they're film stars, and I'm a normal, pigeon-toed, thin-lipped human being. Now editing tools and the freedom to shoot and reshoot are in everyone's hands. We airbrush our own faces and take a thousand different pictures under different lamps until we capture an image that doesn't really look like us and so doesn't make us feel like dog shit. There was not a moment of my adolescence in which I felt happy with how I looked in reality. There were, however, a number of artfully taken photographs in which I thought I looked passable. The existence

---

* According to a 2017 Dove Global Girls, Beauty, and Confidence survey, nine out of ten girls in the UK will avoid seeing friends and family, going out or trying out for teams if they do not feel happy with the way they look.

of these gave me confidence on the internet and decimated my chances of feeling confident in real life.

We want to look as perfect as everyone else, and we want to look as perfect as the perfect versions of ourselves that our phones concoct. This has disastrous consequences.

From 2012 to 2018, the number of admissions to hospital for teens suffering from eating disorders doubled. There are sure to be a number of factors behind this, but social media, most psychologists seem to agree, is unquestionably one of them.

In a study carried out by the Harvard social scientist Leah Somerville, participants were told they were going to be testing a new camera lodged in the head coil of a functional MRI scanner. They were shown a screen that displayed the status of the camera – on, off, or warming up – and told that they were being watched by a member of the same sex roughly the same age as themselves.

The test showed that simply believing they were being looked at was enough to trigger 'emotional, physiological, and neural responses' that were significantly more pronounced in adolescents than in adults or children. These responses included embarrassment, physiological arousal, and MPFC* activation; it seems that our reactions to social evaluation hit a peak in adolescence. The author of the study suggests it may go some way towards explaining why kids do stupid shit when they're with their friends, but I can't help thinking it has some far-reaching implications for how young people use the internet too.

---

* Part of the brain called the medial prefrontal cortex, which has been linked to impulse control, behavioural flexibility, and addiction.

A number of other studies, like variations on the 'cyberball' experiment,* seem to confirm these findings. Adolescents in test settings release more stress hormones when they feel they are under scrutiny. They also report feeling more self-conscious. It appears that there is something specific about the adolescent brain that makes teenagers more susceptible to social evaluation.

Which begs the question, aren't social media sites essentially a way for teenagers to live out Leah Somerville's experiment every hour of the day? And if they're already experiencing a heightened state of self-consciousness, isn't it obvious that posting about yourself and your life will bring you to an unnatural level of self-scrutiny? As someone who is not a neurologist, I can't imagine how exactly this might impact teenage minds. But as someone who owns a human brain, I can assume it's going to be harmful.

How you perceive yourself as a teenager is almost always shaped by how you perceive others. It's obvious that the more you look at pictures of so-called 'beautiful people', the worse you're going to feel about yourself. You will, of course, never measure up to the faces you see in your phone. There are a myriad of studies that link viewing of so-called 'fitspiration' photos on Instagram with low self-worth, body image concerns and eating disorders such as orthorexia and anorexia. This is ostensibly innocent, inspirational content, far removed from

---

* In this experiment, teenagers are led to believe they're playing an online game where they're passing the ball back and forth to another player. Eventually, that player stops passing back. Older adolescents feel a lower mood and greater anxiety than adults and younger adolescents when this happens.

the now infamous 'pro-ana' groups, in which people trade tips and tricks for becoming, and staying, anorexic. By looking at pictures that purport to show them what they could look like, teenagers grow more unhappy with how they actually look.

And this is exactly how 'Instagram influencers' make money. A lot of it. The upper echelons of this burgeoning job sector can receive hundreds of thousands, even millions of dollars for single posts about certain products. They make teenagers feel bad about themselves by posting heavily edited photos of their unnaturally perfect bodies and then sell them products that they claim will bring them up to par.

Lip gloss and trainers and underwear and 'detox tea' that makes you shit until you've lost four kilograms: they are all peddled by influencers who are essentially billboards that young people actively sign up to see.

As is generally the case with celebrity-led advertising, the products are, for the most part, a total con. The make-up on an Instagram celebrity probably looks good because it has been applied by a team of experienced artists, not because it is a marginally different shade from its competitors. Influencers' bodies are inhumanly toned because they have personal trainers and carefully curated meal plans, not because they drink 'affiniTEA' or spend five minutes a week rolling around on an expensive rubber contraption.

This is exactly how Kardashian clan member Kylie Jenner could conjure a billion dollar make-up empire overnight: telling pubescent girls they could look like her if they bought her make-up, despite the fact that, at the very least, she's repeatedly had filler injected into her lips. And it is always the young who are most vulnerable. Advertisers have long targeted teenagers because they are so easy to part from their money. This has not changed, even if the methods have. The difference is that teenagers now seek out adverts, actively devoting hours to staring down at photographs of the rich and famous on their phones, rather than glancing up at giant billboards bearing their faces.

II

Acne has been the scourge of the under-eighteens since there were under-eighteens. Although some studies claim it is the result of living in an age of ice cream sandwiches and acid rain, there are records of people plagued by spots that go as far back as the Egyptians. It appears to be largely genetic rather than the result of external factors, though these can, of course, exacerbate it.

I have suffered this ancient affliction since turning thirteen. What started as a faint archipelago across the forehead became a stubborn mask of painful bumps. Some were deep, red swellings. Others were small, bright whiteheads. Blackheads turned my nose into a strawberry. My forehead felt like the parmesan edge of a cheese grater.

It became worse when it spread down my back. White school shirts very quickly resembled butchers' aprons, so I took to wearing pullovers over them, even in record-breaking summer months. The only consolation lay in squeezing spots onto a mirror I never cleaned, and smearing them like fireworks across the shining sky. At least that offered some sense of accomplishment. That's a big one, I'd think – it'll look pretty on the mirror.

The first time I went to the doctor about my acne, my mum stepped in to offer her diagnosis before our GP could voice hers.

'It's all the chocolate he eats, isn't it?'

'Well,' the doctor said. 'Probably not. There's no proven link between diet and acne.'

My mum pursed her lips and glowered at the doctor. 'But it can't help,' she hissed. 'Can it?'

'It's not a cure, no, but it's not a cause either.'

It should go without saying that I took this as permission to increase my chocolate intake, often replacing whole meals with family-size bars or packets of biscuits. Four other things that I later found out would not cure acne were:

- Toothpaste
- Drinking gallons of water
- Gouging out spots with sewing needles
- Violently scrubbing my face with alcohol-infused pads

But there were also treatments that the doctor offered. Initially antibiotics, which didn't work, followed by a range of creams and lotions. The one that had some effect also hurt like fuck. High-strength benzoyl peroxide is supposed to be introduced to the skin gradually, in small amounts, but in a rush to win the face of my dreams, I plastered my cheeks in it day and night. This dried out my visage to such a degree that for two weeks I routinely pelted to the toilet and dunked it in a sink full of water. This would then cause the benzoyl peroxide to run into my eyes, which would leave them feeling like I'd stared at the sun through binoculars.

It worked for a while until it didn't.

I was eventually referred to a dermatologist. He steepled his fingers and suggested a drug called Roaccutane. It would stop my face producing oil completely, cracking it like a dropped vase. It would mean having to wear sun cream every day. It would have an 80 per cent success rate.

I felt my heart leap.

'It says here you have a suicide attempt,' the dermatologist said.

'I'm feeling a lot better,' I promised. 'I'm taking citalopram.'

'Roaccutane can cause suicidal thoughts.'

'So can the citalopram! As you can see, I'm currently doing a wonderful job of not committing suicide.'

'But do you see what my conundrum is?'

I shook my head.

'I think we ought to try a different form of benzoyl peroxide along with. . .'

I considered saying: I'll kill myself right now if you don't give me Roaccutane.

I did not say this.

I was never given Roaccutane.

The spots eventually diminished but have never fully disappeared.

No one wants acne. There is no positivity movement based off it. Sometimes celebrities pose without make-up, bravely displaying the two miniscule blemishes left behind after two straight weeks of inch-thick make-up worn while filming in the Bahamas, but no one with chronic acne is going to play the lead in a film. I understand: from a continuity perspective, it's difficult to work with acne-ridden actors, but it doesn't do wonders for kids suffering from spots that the only time they see other pizza-faces on the TV is as sickly, cartoonish golems, ambling hunchbacked along behind the proper characters.

Spots wreck one corner of the holy triumvirate of physical goals that the majority of teenagers aspire to and fall short of in one way or another: low body fat percentage, good hair, and clear skin. The problem with them all is how damaging the dogged pursuit of such goals can be. Girls who feel that their spotty skin is unsightly may well daub on inches of Kylie Jenner's make-up that will only end up making it worse. Members of both sexes who are convinced spots are the worst thing ever to happen to a person, will quite likely dig, scratch, pick, and pop their pustules, leaving behind scars that may never go away. Letting children believe that their imperfections are unforgivable may well lead them to ineffective, panicked remedies that will only make things worse. And popped spots are at the mild end of the spectrum, with eating disorders and self-harm growing increasingly prevalent at the other.

III

I doubt teenagers are as interested now in their real-world appearances as they are in their online ones. After all, the internet offers them an audience of millions, while real life consists primarily of parents, siblings, a handful of classmates, and the man who gives you change from a pound for your bag of Magic Stars every morning.

It's traditional for parents to look aghast at what their teenagers are wearing. 'What do you call that?!' 'What have you done to your hair?!' 'What are those things on your feet?!' But from routine observations, it quickly becomes clear that this generation are remarkably conservative in their fashion choices. Few seem to wear anything that makes them stand out in a crowd: no one is wearing anything brighter than khaki, nor are there vast fringes, new make-up patterns or overly ornate pieces of jewellery. There aren't many kids wandering around today who will cringe when they look back on old photos of themselves.

The strangest development might be the newest crop of trainers, soles splayed as though they've been tried on by elephants, but beyond these, current youth fashion trends are unusually tame. The general uniform consists of jeans, joggers, trainers, and hoodies. If you watch a school playground (don't watch a school playground) you'd be hard pressed to pick out groups based on their sartorial choices. There are rarely discernible huddles of differently dressed kids; instead there is one amorphous mass with a handful of brand names scrawled across them.

One of the brands that crops up most often is Supreme. The logo is simply the word Supreme, written in varying fonts across various items. Supreme releases smoke detectors, dominoes, shavers, chopsticks, dog bowls, handcuffs, harmonicas, knives, basketballs, and, primarily, clothes. A Supreme T-shirt will set you back between one hundred and five hundred dollars. A

Supreme fire extinguisher is over a thousand dollars. The clothes tend to be almost breathtakingly plain: crew neck T-shirts with small logos, plain hoodies with small logos, red fire extinguishers with small logos. New clothes are released every single Thursday. Kids camp outside the stores to buy whatever they can grab. Rather than rebellion or shock factor, these kids are seeking authenticity and the chance to own something exclusive. Not necessarily as expensive as name designer brands – at least not initially, though on the resale market prices rise to painful numbers – but difficult to get hold of.

Supreme managed to insert itself into youth culture with similar guerrilla tactics to those that turned cheap plastic headphones labelled Beats by Dre into a billion-dollar company. Rather than whack up billboards and pay for overblown adverts, they make sure their products feature in music videos, paparazzi shots, and Instagram posts. They know that young people do not respond as well to traditional forms of advertising as they do to seeing what kind of toothpaste Billie Eilish is using. It is product placement taken to the extreme: rather than products being positioned strategically into films and TV shows, they are placed into the digital lives of celebrities. Instead of watching George Clooney slurp Nespresso between talk shows on ITV, you see a video of Harry Styles petting a dog while nonchalantly clutching a dick-shaped water bottle. Where did he get that? you think, while scrolling through ten thousand pictures on an iPhone. I simply must have one!

Fashion reflects the mood of the incumbent generation: the idealism of hippies, the nihilism of grunge, the disaffection of skinheads. When punks pushed safety pins through their noses and went to concerts dressed in bin bags, they were making a statement about their anarchic fury. But current fashion seems to lean towards the conservative and utilitarian. It seems to me that teens not only don't particularly want to be seen as different; at a push they want to be considered the same but better. You do not want to parade up and down the pavements drawing attention to yourself when you feel inferior to even the version of yourself that you present to the world via Instagram. The place where you will draw attention to yourself is the internet, not in public. In public, you are the acne-splattered, weak-jawed, tongue-tied idiot that you wish the world would forget about altogether. Online, you control who you are.

No wonder the real world doesn't feel that relevant if you are at your most beautiful inside your phone.

IV

Social media has the potential to be empowering. If you have struggled with self-worth issues, then being able to decide how you're seen can restore a sense of control. One girl I know suffered throughout her early years with an autoimmune disorder which left her skin shedding and her self-esteem in tatters. Taking selfies was a way of getting over the trauma of her illness. In photographs, she could control how she looked, feel beautiful, and receive feedback from others confirming this, thus helping her to slowly rebuild a sense of self-belief.

This is a rare case where the airbrushing tools and filters of apps might come in useful. But generally speaking, developing an online portfolio of carefully shot self-portraits won't do you any favours. Often that cyber confidence functions only as a stand-in. While you might learn to navigate narrow online waters, this may well come at the expense of experience in the open ocean.

At the age of sixteen, I started speaking to a girl on the internet who lived in a town an hour or so away. We spoke most nights for months. The girl posted a lot of pictures with carefully arranged hair, heavy eyeshadow and shorts the length of nappies. She was pretty; she was also fairly interesting and interestingly abrasive.

We eventually decided to meet one Saturday morning in her town. I fidgeted and listened to Eminem on a train for an hour. In panic, I ate fourteen custard creams. I teared up while running a hand over the asphalt of my forehead. Would she think it was disgusting? I'd done a good job of using filters to disguise the acne in photos. Should I have tried to keep our relationship online until I sprouted a beard thick enough to obscure my disappointment of a face?

I imagined a scenario in which I stood alone in a train station for six hours, waiting for a girl who didn't exist; the invention of a bawdy *Warhammer* enthusiast from a half-dead seaside town.

When I got off the train, the girl was standing behind her friend. She did not look at me when I said hello. She remained behind her companion, prodding the friend in the small of her back when there was something she wanted to communicate. It quickly became clear that the confidence lent to her by the filters she used for online photographs did not translate into real life.

For her part, the friend attempted something like jovial conversation. How was your train ride? Which school do you go to? What bands do you like?

We dragged our heels aimlessly around a drizzly, concrete town centre.

We bought cups of coffee in a café affixed to a sports hall.

'Does she not like me?' I asked the friend once the girl had disappeared to the toilet.

'No,' the friend said. 'She really likes you. She's just shy.'

'She hasn't said anything.'

'I told you, she's shy.'

'But we've been talking for ages. And she never came across as shy.'

The friend rolled her eyes. 'She speaks to loads of guys.'

My heart sank. 'Really?'

'Obviously,' said the friend.

The girl returned.

The painful encounter lasted another hour or so. As we said goodbye, she nodded at me then turned and scurried away. I couldn't help thinking she was repulsed by how I looked. I had, after all, spent hours arranging my fringe in photos, then editing them until my acne disappeared and my cheekbones stood out. The real me was a disgusting creature when judged beside his artfully composed online brother. The online version of myself infinitely more lovable.

Against all expectations, a few hours after I got home, the girl started sending messages as though nothing had happened. It was as if there had been nothing unusual in the interaction for her. The internet was where you could talk, real life was not. The internet was where you could feel comfortable in your physicality, the real world was not. She was one of a fairly large number of other pseudo-friends I'd make who had learned to socialize on the computer at the expense of being able to do so in real life.

V

The freedom afforded by the internet could mean an easier way to celebrate diversity. Here is where YouTube can be seen as a beacon of hope. Despite the transgressions committed by its algorithms, the cast of the world's biggest video repository are more diverse than any Hollywood film or sigh-inducing Netflix show. This is because there is no barrier to entry: to participate, all you need is a camera in your room and the ability to wave madly at an invisible audience. As of 2019, of the top ten most subscribed to YouTube channels in the UK, one is a young black musician and vlogger, one is a five-year-old girl who started out making videos for her Romanian family; one is a young woman who leads an all-female gaming group; one is a black, female former investment banker; and one is Alfie Deyes.* Some have interesting things to say, others just want to make money from daring each other to eat cans of cold tuna in front of webcams.

---

* Author of the bestselling *The Pointless Book*, which included such inspiring activities as 'do a finger selfie'. I don't want to cast aspersions on people, because I'm not really sure what aspersions are, but I am not a fan of Alfie Deyes.

There's an opportunity here for parents to take an interest in exactly which rictus-grinning vloggers their offspring are being hypnotized by. It's easy to see YouTube as a single amorphous blob, rather than a complex web of characters, some of whom will prove positive influences and others less so. Crucially though, kids are watching clips from the age of four, and at that age they don't care if their entertainment idols look a certain way. They care if they're funny and good at making food-themed parodies of pop songs. It might seem fairly innocuous, but the wider the variety of faces they see, the broader their idea of what people ought to look like becomes.

In 2013 studies carried out by Jim Pfaus of Syracuse University, rats which experience their first ejaculation while wearing a Velcro vest (to stop them climbing about on each other) would later not be able to have sex unless a Velcro vest was involved. For rats that had humped without a vest, it was impossible to make one vital to their lovemaking. This, Jim claims, points to our sexual tastes being programmed early on. You associate pleasure with a certain look and this look becomes the one you pursue. Of course, sexual attraction isn't the sole measure of beauty, but it is something that is far less innate than we might at first think, at least when it comes to the specifics.

If you grew up in a world populated with a wide array of bodies, it follows that you'd be attracted to and accepting of a wide array of bodies. If you grow up in a world in which only those with turquoise noses are considered beautiful, then of course you're going to spend your time gnawing on your nails in worry over whether your nose is sufficiently turquoise.

I can't help but think that the more kinds of faces and bodies we see as young people, the more kinds of faces and bodies we will find attractive as adults, and the less likely we will be to inadvertently (or advertently) discriminate against others based on appearance. The more open we are to different kinds of beauty, the more accepting we might also be of how we ourselves look.

VI

A few months ago, during a fairly drunken family dinner, my younger half-brother took my younger half-sister's phone and passed it to me. She was on Instagram. I clicked on who she followed and found a number of them described in their bios as 'Victoria's Secret models'. My half-sister is thirteen. Her mum was shocked. She had been convinced that the Instagram account was safe because it was locked, meaning that no one but her approved friends could peer in at her. It is, however, a false mirror: there are no controls on the kind of people she can look out on. There are no controls on the distorted ideas these might give her about how she's supposed to look.

You probably want to give your child freedom. No parent wants to have to spend their free time crouching over their kid's shoulder while they browse through endless pages of garbage on the internet. We know looking at pictures of models isn't going to make anyone happier in their own skin, but presenting your teenager with TV shows and YouTube channels and adverts featuring a broad array of bodies might. Body image issues aren't going to be solved by controlling social media use – there are always going to be photos of skinny blonde women and muscular men around if you want to find them – but by having an ongoing conversation about why we're led to believe certain things are attractive and how we can insulate ourselves against people who will profit off us wanting to look like they do.

It was only when my friend Jenny watched the TV show *Naked Attraction* that she could breathe a sigh of relief that not all vaginas look like the neat, waxed slits she'd glimpsed in snatches of porn. She was twenty-eight. It's a strange weight to carry around, thinking your vagina is imperfect compared to everyone else on the planet.

'They hang down,' she said, amazed.

'Well,' I said, 'yeah. Some of them hang down.'

'You knew that?'

'Of course.'

'Why didn't you tell me?'

'I thought you knew.'

'How would I know?'

It had taken *twenty-eight* whole years for her to find out that not all female vaginas resembled those of Barbies. Maybe nudists are on to something.

Don't forget:

- Know who your kids are following on Instagram. It's not enough to know their account is private: what they're looking out on can be as damaging as who's looking in.

- Watch films together where people are naked. Watch *Naked Attraction* if you have to. The more imperfect, normal human bodies young people see, the more comfortable they'll feel in their own skin.

- If they ask for something, ask them why they want it, and if it transpires that they want it because Selena Gomez posted a picture of herself holding it, then have a discussion about what that means. Selena Gomez didn't make it and she doesn't really use it – someone just paid her to hold it for six seconds, quadrupling its cost.

Homework:

Time to try out Instagram. If you haven't got it, you'll need to make an account. Once you do, you can start posting artfully shot photos of your dinners, shoes, and crying jags. Try searching for things like 'fitspiration' or 'lifegoals' or 'brexitmeansbrexit' and see what comes up.

Lesson Nine:

Go Swimming

Self-harm and bad romance

I

As a parent, it can often feel impossible to say anything that will get through to your teenager. You can almost see your son's brain shutting down while you talk, disregarding everything that comes out of your mouth. 'Are you listening to me?' Your daughter nods, eager for the exchange to be over. Once you've finished, they'll reconvene with friends and explain their lateness by way of Mum refusing to shut up.

'About what?'

'I don't know, some shit.'

Your child will listen to Tekashi 6ix9ine, food-related podcasts, and interviews in which the gender pay gap is dissected, but they will not listen to you. But when you feel like none of the words you choose are right, it doesn't mean there isn't a right way of doing things. Or a wrong way.

Never was this clearer to me than when, at the age of fourteen, my mother discovered a diary chronicling months of self-harm. Rather than come to me, she chose to share it with the head of my year at school. I was pulled out of a lesson without warning and taken to the Corridor of Serious Offices, where only the most high-ranking teachers lived. I do not know why she thought a childless, middle-aged geography teacher would be any more adept at handling the issue than her. All I know is that, unlike the doctor's surgery, she was not present during my interrogation.

I guess she'd panicked.

From the conversations I've had around me in the last few years, self-harm seems to be a uniquely modern problem that remains virtually incomprehensible to the preceding generation. In his book *Capitalist Realism*, Mark Fisher claims that it isn't wildly off the mark to say that being a teenager in late-capitalist Britain is 'close to being reclassified as a sickness'. Whether there is any direct link between thumbing through Twitter for five hours a day and gouging chunks out of your thigh is difficult to determine. What is not difficult to determine is the scale of the problem. According to research in the *Lancet Psychiatry*, the prevalence of self-harm amongst women aged sixteen to twenty-four rose from 6.5 per cent in 2000 to 19.7 per cent in 2014. Figures from the Office for National Statistics for 2018 showed that teenage suicide in England and Wales increased by 67 per cent between 2010 and 2017. In 1986, the year of Childline's conception, there were no calls about self-harm. By 2018, nearly a quarter of the UK's fifteen-year-old girls had reported purposely hurting themselves. If you start looking for scars up the arms of the under-thirties, you'll see them.

Back in my geography teacher's dim office, I was not offered a cup of tea before our impromptu tête-à-tête began. I understand that children are not commonly offered cups of tea in schools, but I really think that sometimes it would help. As we discussed in the tea interlude, there are scientific studies that show how having something warm between your hands makes you happier, more amenable, and less susceptible to negative thoughts. He wouldn't have even had to make the tea, I would have happily done it myself. (I leave this discovery here for the benefit of school-age readers, should they have stolen their parents' copy of this book: the taps in art rooms are often made super-hot for getting paint off palettes more easily – hot enough, in fact, for the making of tea. I have tested this theory successfully, in three separate secondary schools.)

'Do you know what this is about?' the geography teacher asked.

I thought for a bit. I knew it could have been about smoking, selling drugs, unexplained absences, or stealing books from the library. Even then, I thought it was rather sneaky to open with that question as a tactic for garnering more information, like he was hoping to catch a confession for some other crime while investigating this one. I decided not to give him what he wanted.

'No, sir.'

'No idea?'

'I don't think so.'

And out of his desk comes the dog-eared exercise book I

had pilfered from the maths cupboard a few months earlier. I had drawn a crucified bunny rabbit on the front cover, trails of red blood oozing out of its hands and feet. The pages inside contained rants about the meaninglessness of life, the impossibility of free will, and the shape of Jessica Dennet's coccyx. The more damning elements of the tome involved the frequency and seriousness of self-harm, much of which sounded suspiciously like a certain Nine Inch Nails song made famous by a certain dead country singer*.

I clammed up. The notebook was supposed to be under my pillow. That was where it lived. It only came out late at night, when I was feeling lonely, and now it was between the meaty hands of my head of year.

'Would you like to read some of this to me?' he asked.

'No.'

'Go on.'

'I don't want to read it,' I said. 'I know what it says.'

'And what does it say?'

'Nothing.'

'Can you think why we might be worried?'

'No.'

'Go on and read it.'

'I'm not going to read it.'

'Read it.'

'No.'

---

* If you're feeling a little maudlin, you might want to head to YouTube and watch the video for Johnny Cash's cover of 'Hurt'.

'Read it.'

'Stop saying that, sir.'

'That isn't how you talk to a teacher.'

'I don't want to be talking to a teacher.'

'Well, I don't want my pupils to be injuring themselves, so we're a bit at loggerheads, aren't we?'

I was made to roll up the sleeves of my shirt until the cuts were visible.

'Why would you want to do that to yourself?'

Shrug, shrug, eye roll.

'Help me to understand.'

Shrug, shrug, eye roll, shrug. Sigh, sigh.

'You'll have to talk to someone, even if you don't want to talk to me.'

'I don't want to talk to someone.'

'It wasn't a question. You're a good lad, don't go messing everything up.'

'I'm not hurting anyone.'

'You're hurting yourself.'

'Hardly. It hardly hurts.'

'Why do it?'

Shrug, shrug, sigh.

'Will you stop doing it?'

'Stop doing what?'

'You know . . .' (Gestures vaguely, as though he's chopping a carrot.)

'Yes, sir.'

'Do you promise?'

'Absolutely.'

'All right. You can go. But I'll be keeping this and you have to stop stealing notebooks.'

Surprising as it might seem, I failed to keep this promise. I shrugged off questions from my mum during dinner, went to my bedroom, logged on, jerked off to a threesome, and retraced a few old cuts on the upper arms with my compass.

Usually I used rough utensils that could be dragged back and forth, over and over, rather than sharp objects that would cut more easily. Obviously there are a thousand other ways to self-harm. Someone might continually pick holes in their scalp or scratch open the skin on their face or hands. Someone might tug out their hair. Someone might whack themselves with hard objects. Someone might fist-fight a brick wall until their knuckles swell and burst.

Some kids are opportunistic in their self-harming, while others have especially set-aside kits made up of razor blades and anti-septic wipes. Some do it in purposely visible places, others make sure to hide every mark.

Teenagers self-harm in school toilets, under desks, under duvets, in the morning, in the night, at break time, whenever certain memories crop up, during highs, during lows, and during lulls. Self-harm can become a strange and lonely ritual that resembles taking drugs. It can even *feel* like taking drugs and become as addictive as anything that can be put up your nose.

The one thing that most forms of self-harm have in common is that Bepanthen seems to be thoroughly useful when dealing with almost all resulting ailments. Bepanthen should be kept handy.

It is both soothing and antiseptic. When faced with a self-harm wound, apply Bepanthen.

II

You're likely wondering: why would a teenager self-harm? Do they think this is a cool thing to do? Are they really that misguided? Did I, their doting parent, at some point in their infancy drop them head first onto a tiled floor?

The reasons are probably as varied as the methods. For some, learning of the existence of self-harm will in itself be enough to prompt them to try it. Young people are pathologically curious. If they learn about something that other people are doing, there's a fair chance they'll want to try it: this is how the internet convinced children to eat washing machine tablets and choke on fistfuls of cinnamon.*

For others, I think there are probably a few common triggers that might lead you down the path to self-mutilation. My best guesses are:

- Inadequacy: Teenagers feel like shit all the time and this is a way of confirming to themselves that they're shit. This might go some way towards explaining why girls are more

---

* The great cinnamon challenge of 2007–2012 involved eating a spoonful of ground cinnamon in under one minute without drinking any liquid. On camera, of course. At least one boy died from asphyxiation as a result. Don't say this generation haven't fought their wars.

severely affected. It is surely nigh on impossible to feel comfortable in yourself as a teenage girl in the third millennium AD, when you're supposed to be neither virginal nor slutty, unconventional looking nor obsessed with appearance, shy nor outspoken, fat nor thin, smart nor stupid.

- Control: I remember that, at fifteen, I felt ready to exist independently in the world. I felt ready for my own private life, complete with my own flat and bathtub and choice of breakfast cereal. But I was made to be in my bedroom by ten, often surrender my phone, and spend entire days being told to tuck in my shirt. Here, finally, was something I could control. It wasn't much, but it was mine.

- Escape: The world always feels too small before you're properly released into it. Life is always happening elsewhere. Life is always happening to other people. When teens hurt themselves, they're somewhere else, somewhere that isn't normal life.

- Chemical release: Physical pain causes the releases of endorphins* as the body's way of trying to help you out and keep the worst of it at bay. For a brain struggling with turmoil, a little dose of biological Nurofen is always welcome.

- Attention: As a way of calling out for help, this is a bright flare sent up from the pits of despair.

---

* Endorphin is a contraction of 'endogenous morphine', our own personal supply of the good stuff.

- Everything: Any and all of the above might appear in isolation but might also exist as a symptom of diagnosable mental illness. There have long been arguments about whether to treat certain things as symptoms or as issues in themselves (insomnia, for example). I don't know the answer to that and it feels like something that's beyond my remit.

If I try to pick apart why I wanted to hurt myself, I blush. At the time, I remember occupying a sort of moral high ground about self-harming. I was not doing it to be seen to be doing it, I reasoned. Not like Emma, who digs into her forearms and wears short-sleeved tops, or Kat who has near-enough cut the word 'help' into her forehead.

Of course, I did want it to be noticed; I just didn't want it noticed that I wanted noticing. The only difference was that I thought there was a difference. I also wanted to prove I was unhappy, even though on the surface there was little or nothing to be unhappy about. It was a way of showing in concrete terms an internal commotion that I knew would be brushed aside if it was voiced. I knew that my mum would put air quotes around depression and point out that the rest of the world managed to get by just fine. This steadfast belief would keep her from acknowledging that even she was not, in fact, managing to get by just fine. Like a lot of people of her generation, she felt so sure that mental health problems weren't 'a thing' that she refused to see them even in herself.

But that's another book.

III

There's another attraction to self-harming. While cutting, I would communicate with a number of girls online or by text, comparing when we'd last cut ourselves, with what and how many times. There was something like comradeship in this. 'Used a razor for the first time,' someone would text. 'Tried an unfolded paperclip during maths' or 'dabbed a pinch of salt into the cut'.

It felt good to be sharing the experience. There was, of course, an element of wanting to belong to a subset of people, however illogical their unifying mission. It was a way of fitting in, but more significantly, it was all shrouded in an irresistible cloak of romanticism.

Romanticizing things is sometimes a coping mechanism in itself. If you find yourself in a fucked-up, horrible place, then connecting it to something larger and more beautiful can provide the energy needed to carry on. By romanticizing something, you can give it a clearer form, and understand it as part of a story. And the internet is the perfect place for this to happen.

There are long corridors of the internet hung with photographs that romanticize the act of self-harm: roses artfully arranged around bleeding cuts, melodramatic poems written over photographs of scabs, cigarette smoke coiled around razor scars. This is clearly a difficult situation, and, as I'm writing this, Instagram have just clamped down on images of what they call 'self-injury'. It's not hard to see why: the idea of kids scrolling through tastefully lit pictures of open wounds and then replicating that effect on themselves is terrifying.

The acne years are when you're at the pinnacle of romanticism. You discover the music you'll hold dear for the rest of your life, music you'll scream along to alone in cars, the music that you'll one day bellow at your kids is 'real music'. You'll discover books that you'll lug between every mildewed flat of your adult life. You'll watch and re-watch the films that will sculpt your vocabulary.

You look for stories and you adopt them as your own because you haven't yet had the life experiences to create your own. Slowly, through a process of emulation and refinement, you discover what you think, what you make of the world, and how you see yourself in it. But until that moment, the impulse to try a new thing is overpowering, and when there's a narrative surrounding it that makes you look and feel deep, tortured, and interesting, then it's completely seductive.

The question, when this meets self-harm, really becomes: is your daughter relating to someone else because they cut themselves, or is she cutting herself to relate to someone else? What comes first, the self-harm or the romanticization of it? The answer is probably different for different people and it's possible that it doesn't matter.

When I was in the throes of depression, I liked thinking about the lives of deranged teenaged poets like Arthur Rimbaud and Percy Bysshe Shelley. These syphilitic boys suffered from feeling invisible, torn apart, empty, pointless, terrified, and already dead, and they expressed these feelings in grand, serious poems that are still foisted on unsuspecting schoolchildren today. Their spells of wild hopelessness and despair were shaped into works of art. Whether it was good art or not, it didn't matter. What mattered was that they had felt the way I was feeling.

It gave me a well-established framework in which I could situate unprecedented feelings while I spent whole nights sitting on my windowsill, pissing on myself, over and over, until the sun came up. Come morning, I would put on dry boxers and get back into bed and shiver. This was too much to comprehend from where I was standing. It was too pathetic, too upsetting, and too lonely. But with a dose of romance, I could convince myself that I wasn't an embarrassing, disgusting little creature. I could belong to that age-old tradition of young people feeling like they'd fallen off a passing spaceship. The sadness was a tangible presence, a spectre that had been making unwanted visits to pale introverts for hundreds of years.

Urinating on oneself and having a go at your arms with old steak knives is relatively harmless, but romanticizing other more serious acts of self-harm can obviously lead to tragedy. It becomes a particularly dangerous line of thought when it comes to things like suicide (which, you'll be thrilled to hear, we'll be covering in the next chapter). As a young person, it is easy to get lost in fantasies of mournful schoolmates, guilt-wracked enemies, and tearful crushes. There must always be a firm tether to reality otherwise it can become difficult to find one's way back.

IV

I carried on self-harming because it was never dealt with. My encounter with the geography teacher achieved just one thing: I stopped stealing notebooks. With my parents, self-harm became an embarrassing, untalked-about thing that was sometimes flung about as an accusation during arguments. I continued to cut, drink, and cry. This generally involved scratching bloody holes into the backs of my hands and fore-arms or punching walls until my knuckles swelled up and split open.* Increasingly, the driving factor felt more like rage than sadness. It was still a way of replacing overwhelming emotion with a simply understood feeling. It was, at least for a brief period of time, like consolidating all of your loans into one simple monthly repayment.

I don't know what I wish my mum had done when she found the diary with the crucified bunny on it. I know, really, that any attempts at discussing the matter would have been met with either indifference or outright hostility. I would not have said anything honest about what I was feeling or doing to myself.

What would have helped would have been the chance to talk to, watch or read about someone who had been in the same place, and no longer was. I know that now. Cutting yourself alone in your room is isolating, that's why I was speaking about it to other kids

---

* Such a widespread occurrence that 'white boys punching walls' has become a kind of mocking meme in itself.

who cut. The problem is, we were all so deep into it, we couldn't see the wood for the trees.

It would have helped to have been ushered into assembly one morning with a relatively normal looking twenty-year-old standing up on stage.

'Yes, I was in that place,' they would say, 'and I realized it wasn't helping, and with support and an arsenal of coping techniques I overcame it. If I wanted the same feeling of release, I munched ice cubes or lifted weights or ran until my blisters burst. I listened to loud music. I took up kickboxing. When I felt like cutting, I found one person that I could text and tell, and that person would call and force me to promise to come over and re-watch *Mary Poppins* or burp through two-litres of Coke and a bucket of chicken wings.'

I realize this is probably beyond achievable in most cases. It is idealistic. How do you find an ex-self-harmer willing to address ornery fifteen-year-olds? Newspaper adverts?

Did you use to self-mutilate? Have you since given it up and embarked on an exciting career? Are you capable of inspiring speeches? Can you dodge small paper missiles and ignore over four hundred pairs of eyes audibly rolling at your presence?

Maybe this is already happening, I don't know. Let's hope it becomes a normal occurrence in schools all over the country. There is a reason so much of modern addiction recovery is based not on talking to psychiatrists, but on listening to other addicts who have sober years under their belts – these are the people who can best understand the situation, while simultaneously offering proof that life can and will be better once you've managed to overcome your obstacle.

In the meantime, if you discover your child is self-harming, it's easy for the first reaction to be anger. What is wrong with you? Why are you doing this to yourself? Would you key your own car? Smash your own TV? I've done everything to give you a fulfilling start to life, and you sit up in your room wounding yourself. What does it mean? That you hate yourself? That the life I've given you isn't good enough? What have I done wrong? Where did I fail?

It is likely that you will convince yourself the idea of self-harming came from a less than savoury friend of your perfect child. This is totally normal. Very few people want to consider the possibility of their own kids acting out of free will when it comes to upsetting behaviour. It is easier to banish nasty friends than it is to reckon with your child's intense feelings of worthlessness or despair.

It is also less effective, let me tell you: it is important you have the difficult conversation. Having said that, you need to get the tone right. Once again – and I can't say this often enough – don't lose your shit, and don't bombard them with probing questions once you've calmed down. There is a danger that in interrogating a teenager too thoroughly about self-harm you can make them feel stupid and ashamed, which is slightly counterproductive because those two emotions might already have enough of a starring role in their lives. Half of the time they will have no clue why they've done what they've done; the other half of the time, they won't want to talk about it, which is exactly why they carved up their calves instead. Clearly, it shouldn't go unexamined, but it also shouldn't be investigated like a crime.

Sometimes, when my comrades in self-harm and I were deep in discussion about how our passions were playing out, one of them might disappear without warning. You knew what had happened: their mum had stumbled across a phone loaded with incriminating text messages and confiscated it indefinitely. It's hard to believe that further social isolation helped them in many ways. At least the phone had been a distraction from dissecting their biceps. Now what was left to do?

If you're looking for signs that your teenager is self-harming, consider not trawling through their phone. Again, it has the possibility of igniting a mistrust that can close down channels of communication which might one day be needed. When I found out my phone was being looked at, I narrowed my eyes, surrendered it to Mum, and bought my own second-hand one. From then on, I kept it near me at all times. If it was ever confiscated as a punishment, I'd be sure to prise out the SIM card first. I would like to suggest a less risky way of discovering whether your child is self-harming: take them swimming. You'll be able to see their bodies without subjecting them to a humiliating strip search. While they're likely to try and sprint from the changing room into the water, you'll probably get at least a glimpse of their upper arms and legs.

Once you have confirmation, the worst possible cause of action is to belittle a person who self-harms, intentionally or not. Don't say they're just doing it for attention, because if a young person wants attention so badly that they're willing to inflict serious physical pain on themselves then it might be time to give them some. And the right kind of attention. Not the kind of attention that makes them want to press harder on the penknife and lop off an entire limb, but the kind that says, yes, I can see that you're struggling, and I want to help in whichever way makes you comfortable, without judgement.

You could encourage them to talk to someone, and it doesn't even have to be in person if they don't want. There are Skype counsellors, anonymous ones. There are youth-focused mental health apps like Kooth, which involve peer-to-peer interaction as well as counselling. And you can reassure them that they don't have to tell you anything about it if they don't want to. Support and human connection are the obvious antidotes to many of the causes of self-harm, but it's vital that they take forms that are comfortable for those involved.

Like everyone else on the planet, I wish that any problems I'd had could have been seen without being stated. I wanted to be understood without having to make myself understood. I wanted, deep down, to be driven to a calm and thoughtful counsellor and given a hug and a book token.

Once, a friend, upon seeing a fresh set of weeping holes on my left hand, very sweetly instructed me to sit down while he produced a tube of antibacterial cream and gently spread it on my punctured skin. He did not ask why the wounds were freakishly evenly spaced or why the fingernails of one hand were bright red. He suggested we listen to some music then go out for breakfast, which we did. This was far better than the question: 'What have you done to yourself?' Or being grunted at through a crumb-specked moustache by a bewildered geography teacher.

Don't forget:

- Self-harm always means something. Whether it's the symptom of a mental health problem, an attempt to fit in, or a cry for help, it is not something that can be ignored.
- By all means seek outside advice but ask a teenager first whether they'd prefer to speak to you or to someone else about what's going on. You may well feel unqualified to talk about it, but letting a young person feel like they have some control over who they confide in is vital.
- Stay calm. I know I've already said that, but I'm saying it again. You getting riled up, either out of anger, fear, frustration, or whatever else, is not going to help anyone. It would be like standing and screaming in the aftermath of a car crash, rather than trying to help the wounded.

Homework:

If you search #noharmdone on YouTube, you'll find a number of useful videos created by the charity Young Minds, in which parents and teenagers openly discuss their experiences of self-harm. They'll show you that not only is it a common phenomenon, it's a beatable one.

Interlude 4:

Reading List for Panicked Parents

Here are some suggestions for novels and pieces of non-fiction that I think would help me if I ever found myself saddled with providing for a couple of half-baked humans who preferred YouTube to exchanging three sentences with their dear father:

The Teenage Brain: A Neuroscientist's Survival Guide to Raising Adolescents and Young Adults, **Frances E. Jensen and Amy Ellis Nutt**

As mentioned in chapter 2. I liked this book a lot even if I found a fair number of reasons to roll my eyes. There are a few other almost identical books[*] that say the same things, namely pointing to which areas of the brain are underdeveloped in teenagers, and

---

[*] *Brainstorm: The Power and Purpose of the Teenage Brain* by Daniel Siegel, *Blame My Brain* by Nicola Morgan, and *Inventing Ourselves: The Secret Life of the Teenage Brain* by Sarah-Jayne Blakemore.

how this can explain their mood swings, inability to communicate, and talent for doing stupid shit.

The Circle, Dave Eggers

A warning about the impact on our personal lives of ubiquitous social media.

Generation Z: Their Voices, Their Lives, Chloe Combi

This book is a collection of testimonies from teenagers around Britain. It's a thoroughly interesting read, if sometimes harrowing.

Emergency Contact, Mary H.K. Choi

A YA novel that shows the power a virtual relationship can have to keep people afloat in difficult times.

You Are Not a Gadget, Jaron Lanier

Jaron Lanier was one of the architects of the internet as we know it, and this is his warning about the deleterious effects the modern iteration of the internet will have on us as human beings and as a culture.

Bookworm, A Memoir of Childhood Reading, Lucy Mangan

A testament to the power books can have to inject magic and meaning into chaotic childhoods.

Night Falls Fast, Kay Redfield Jamison

One of the most haunting and illuminating books on suicide I've read, it focuses largely on suicide amongst the young.

Drink? The New Science of Alcohol and Your Health,
Professor David Nutt
An honest, if overly straightforward book about alcohol's impact
on us and how it compares to other drugs.

Get Out of My Life . . . But First Take Me and Alex into
Town, **Suzanne Franks**
A slightly outdated London-centric book that still has a number
of practical tips for teenager-rearing. Also, it's a good title. I
remember once walking with a friend to his house when his mum
pulled up next to us, wound down her window, and gently asked
if we'd like a lift home.

'GO AWAY, MUM!' he screamed.

When she drove off, he turned to me and said, 'She's such a
bitch.'

The first thing he said to her when we got there was: 'Can you
make us a sandwich?'

Lesson Ten:

Suicide

Meditation, selfishness, and Netflix

I

A few days ago, I saw a friend of a friend post on Facebook that he was sorry for what he was about to do. He wrote about feeling tired, alone, and defeated. The post ended with: 'I have decided to end my own life by jumping off a bridge in the next few hours'. I sat and watched as hundreds of comments accumulated below the post. People gave their phone numbers, offered to buy plane tickets, suggested holidays and meet-ups and new coffee shops they could visit together. Distant relatives arranged for other people to go to his house. Two people called an ambulance, another called the police. Several promised to watch bridges in his area. Friends told him he mattered, had a life ahead of him, had inspired them and helped them and shown them kindness when the rest of the world didn't.

It was impossible to tell whether he was still receiving those comments.

I wondered if he was currently looking down at a river, watching his feet dangle in the air. I wondered if he was already dead.

A little later, someone posted a comment saying they had gone to his house and kicked down the door. He wasn't there. He'd left without his phone or wallet. He hadn't, it seemed, read any of the heartfelt messages people had left under his status.

More comments said they were wandering the area looking for him.

Even more comments asked if there was any news.

Finally, someone posted one saying that they had found him and taken him to the nearest mental health facility. The last flare in his gun had been spotted before the ship went down.

II

We didn't talk about suicide back in the chapter about mental health because it's huge and complicated and delicate and I don't know how to do it. I'm not a trained professional, which a number of people think means I shouldn't talk about it at all. But I have at least attempted suicide (not, you might have guessed, successfully).

I'm not alone. Data from the Office for National Statistics shows that suicides amongst British fifteen-to-seventeen-year-olds hit an all-time high in 2015 and the second highest in 2017. The act of killing oneself, especially in young people, can be chillingly unpredictable. There might be the deepening of recognizable symptoms of depression, but there might be no warning whatsoever. You can keep an eye out for signs of distress, but what if one day Oscar's friends decide to spread a rumour that he's got one ball, and his undeveloped brain convinces him that this is a shadow he'll never manage to crawl out of. I have to kill myself, he thinks. There's no way things are going to get better now.

All too often, this is how it happens. As a young person, you can barely see beyond the horizon. The hyper-instantaneity of the modern world does nothing to help someone in a dark place believe that there will be a tomorrow and another tomorrow and another tomorrow after that, all of them different shades of despair, joy, and boredom. You forget, very easily, that school is only practice for life, that it isn't the start and end of everything. You are incredibly susceptible to apocalyptic thoughts. It does not take much to convince you that your world is over.

According to a 2007 Houston study of 153 survivors of suicide, around 75 per cent of suicide attempts were deliberated over for less than an hour, with 24 per cent of those thought about for less than five minutes. What this means is that in many cases you're unlikely to get a chance to catch someone in the time between the idea of suicide arriving in their head and their attempt at it. This is why it is so crucial to drill in survival techniques to any teenager who has experienced emotional trouble before they attempt suicide.

It is why hotlines and social media are so vital. Even five minutes is long enough to scoop out your phone and type 0800 1111 or tweet that you need help, though it might not be long enough to summon the courage necessary to speak directly to a person you know. Apps like notOK, developed by a pair of teenage siblings from Georgia, USA, can function as panic buttons, where one tap will alert a preselected group of family and friends to your location and need for help.

But the biggest armour against suicide – and I'm not talking about suicide in the midst of mental illness, rather the more impulsive breed of teenage suicide that tends to be an exaggerated response to some mild trauma – is teaching someone not to trust their thoughts. 'Why am I thinking this?' 'Where did the thought come from?' 'Can I trust it?' The sooner kids start being critical of their own thoughts, the easier it will be for them to climb out from under them.

The best way is to try and instil in your kids early on the idea that thoughts often have little connection to reality. Don't believe everything you think. The idea that everything is terrible and won't get better is just that: an idea, a terrible one, akin to porn passports or becoming a professional YouTuber. You got a D in that essay on symbolism in *King Lear*, remember? You thought Cordelia was meant to be winter and her dying would usher in the spring. You have terrible ideas all the time, Oscar. You have to learn to keep them from taking the reins and start to work out a way of separating them from your better ones, ones like the school strike for climate change or getting a dumbphone or keeping a dream diary.

This, in essence, is the primary goal of cognitive behavioural therapy: to recognize harmful and negative thoughts and feelings, then do something about them. The more they're aware of this, the more likely they'll be to be capable of taking a step back and try to work out the best course of action.

III

In 2016, a nineteen-year-old French girl named Oceane sat in front of her webcam, streaming video of herself smoking cigarettes. She was using a live-streaming app called Periscope. As she smoked, comments flashed past. They were mostly jokey and light, despite what the girl was saying.

Oceane told the viewers she was going to kill herself. She explained that she had been raped and went on to give the name of her attacker. She said she wasn't doing it for attention, but to open people's eyes to what this person had done.

No one in the comments really thought she would kill herself. The internet can be seen as one unending repository of empty threats. I'll kill myself! thousands cry. Of course you will, come the replies.

But as the viewers continued to watch, Oceane continued to stream, carrying her phone to the nearby train station of Égly, south of Paris.

Those watching scrambled to alert emergency services. The next thing they saw was a policeman's face as he picked up Oceane's phone. She was dead.

Live-streamed suicides are the logical outcome of lives lived online. If you share everything else with the internet, why would you not share this?

IV

'No doubt you are right, my best of friends,' wrote Goethe in *The Sorrows of Young Werther*, 'there would be far less suffering amongst mankind, if men – and God knows why they are so fashioned – did not employ their imaginations so assiduously in recalling the memory of past sorrow, instead of bearing their present lot with equanimity.'

Young Werther is a serious, melodramatic man who falls in love with a woman who is already engaged. Things do not go well. Werther wanders around feeling shitty, eventually goes to see the woman one last time, then shoots himself in the head and is buried beneath a lime tree. After the book was published, there were reports that young men were both dressing like Werther – in blue jackets, boots, and yellow trousers – and putting bullets through their brains like Werther too. This became known as the Werther Effect, or copycat suicide.

It is a phenomenon that is still bickered over today. How do we report suicides? Is there a duty to the truth or to the general public? Can stories incite suicide? Does that mean we shouldn't tell them?

At the beginning of 2017, Netflix released a show called *Thirteen Reasons Why*, based on the book by Jay Asher. It revolves around the suicide of a girl named Hannah, who leaves behind a box of cassette tapes implicating those she has left behind. Each character listens to the tapes, learns Hannah's story and their role in it, and feels extremely terrible about themselves. How could I have been so thoughtless! they think. How could I have treated that dear-departed angel so callously!

In the wake of the TV show, online searches for 'how to kill yourself' jumped up, and some sources suggested that suicide rates amongst American males had increased by up to 30 per cent. In Britain, a twelve-year-old girl hanged herself three weeks after it was first shown, leaving behind a list of 'six reasons to kill myself'.

The reason that *Thirteen Reasons Why* is such an unnecessary and dangerous piece of shit to show young people is because it shows a person getting exactly what they wanted after their death: everyone to feel guilty and run around thinking about them non-stop. Hannah's suicide is, to all intents and purposes, a successful act of revenge. This plays into fantasies that many emotionally overwhelmed teenagers harbour.

I'll show them, they think. I'll make them sorry they ever called me bubble-butt. I know these were the kinds of thoughts that contributed at least in part to every time I half-heartedly tried to kick the bucket. You feel, on some level, that by killing yourself you'll finally be able to prove your pain to those around you. You'll prove how sad, how right, and how unappreciated you were.

It is a bad idea to show young people stories in which suicides play out exactly as the person committing suicide intends. That is so obvious it's surprising it needs to be said at all. *The Sorrows of Young Werther* could have predicted this. Any reasonable psychologist could have predicted this. Any survivor of a teenage suicide attempt could have predicted this. Netflix, apparently, could not. It plods along, commissioning virtually everything that is offered to it with the sixteen billion dollars it generates every year.

Thirteen Reasons Why is the pinnacle of the worst kind of romanticization. It is exploiting a daydream that many young people already drift towards, to such an extent that it has surely nudged at least one kid off a cliff. I struggle to see how you could make a case for it exploring issues around mental health and suicide through the prism of revenge and guilt. Oh, how they'll weep when you're gone! it says. Oh, how they'll realize what a wonderful person you were when it's too late!

We know what the problem of Netflix is: it is competing with no one. Young people, when they choose to watch professionally produced content rather than self-directed YouTube videos, almost exclusively watch Netflix. It is not like terrestrial TV, where channels compete for your attention by writing and producing content they hope is better than that of their competitors. If you don't like something on Netflix, you watch something else on Netflix. If the newer rival services fail to gain a sufficient foothold, it may become the sole portal through which the youth consume TV and films, both old and new, and this means it has a giant responsibility to treat them and the issues they're wrestling with decently. It cannot afford to be clumsy with content aimed at young people. It cannot be allowed to casually put out programmes for children about suicide, as though it is just another subject ripe for ten hours of internet-TV mediocrity.

V

The media has tried to alter its reporting of suicide over the past decade in an effort to deter copycat acts, but the internet has no such conscience. Neither do musicians. The late nineties and early 2000s saw a boom in emo music, a kind of middle ground between punk and rock where self-harm, sadness, and suicide were the main lyrical topics.

In recent years, certain rappers have taken on the mantle of spokespeople for the mentally unwell. In the same way certain rappers once adopted the personas of hardened criminals, many now rap about being anxious, depressed, or otherwise emotionally unbalanced. This ties back in with the idea of suffering conferring a certain realness and worth to a person. The privilege of mental stability is sometimes thought of like the privilege of wealth or class: it can be seen as a marker of inauthenticity.

When Lil Peep rapped about dreaming of suicide it resonated, because it has always helped young people to hear their feelings reflected back at them through music. What they need to be reminded of is how much of these songs and personas are acts: not all of the late-eighties rappers who sang about selling crack ever really sold crack, not all of the current rappers who claim to be considering suicide really are. They are not, very often, in the same position you are. They are chasing a trend. They are creating an image.

Of course, young people need to be aware that suicide happens, but they don't need to watch it happen, again and again, in mediums that give the illusion of life going on after they die.

As with a number of other behaviours, there is the question: if a child had not learned in detail about suicide, would they be attempting it? Is it something they would naturally feel their way to in the darkness? Or is it something that can be removed from the arsenal of human behaviours altogether?

Dan Everett is an American linguist who has spent a great deal of time living with the Pirahã people of the Amazon basin. He initially went to them as a missionary, bent on introducing the holy word of Jesus into their otherwise savage lives. He claims that after finding them happier, healthier, and more social than he's ever been, he dropped the Bible stuff and started trying to learn from the Pirahã instead of preaching to them.

In one story he tells about his time with the tribe, Everett remembers giving a sermon to the Pirahã about his stepmother. He explained to them that she had become incredibly depressed, so depressed in fact that she one day killed herself with a gunshot to the head. When he reached this point in the story, the Pirahã burst out laughing.

From a transcript of the *Freakonomics* podcast:

EVERETT: *When I asked them why are you laughing, they said: 'She killed herself. That's really funny to us. We don't kill ourselves. You mean, you people, you white people shoot yourselves in the head? We kill animals, we don't kill ourselves.' They just found it absolutely inexplicable, and without precedent in their own experience that someone would kill themselves.*

The most helpful thing you could do as a parent is de-romanti-cize suicide. Here are two scenarios you might use: someone gets very close to suicide but manages to reach out and access help, thus improving their life; or someone commits suicide and sure, the people at school cry for one day, and after that most of them move on with their lives – lives that are filled with unexpected joys and terrors and loves and losses, lives that are long and full, lives in which the suicided person is nothing but a half-remembered footnote.

So keep an eye on what they're watching through Netflix. And YouTube. The creators making their money out of those mediums may not possess the same sense of conscience we've come to expect from traditional media outlets.

VI

At the age of fifteen I ditched school, got a train across England, walked six miles down country lanes and began a five-day silent meditation retreat at a Buddhist monastery. You had to be eighteen to participate and you had to sign a form saying you would adhere to the five precepts of Buddhism, one of which is: don't lie. I signed the form. I didn't mind lying, especially not to a religion. I wasn't particularly interested in the Buddhist accoutrements of the retreat, just the benefits of meditation, which I had read were starting to accrue some scientific support.

For the five days you weren't allowed to speak, you were given one small vegetarian meal per day, you had to sleep on the floor, you had to wake up at 4.30 a.m., and you had to participate in around eight hours of meditation per day. Three people left before the five days were up. I struggled but made it, experiencing moments that felt, to me at least, like something profound.

The real change came afterwards. I returned home in a state my sister described as 'freaky'. I was incredibly calm and quiet. I noticed everything. I felt things very keenly. Over the following weeks I found that I noticed my thoughts and feelings in a different way to the usual. Oh, I'd think – look, I'm feeling angry. Why am I feeling angry? Where has that come from? This self-awareness faded as I failed to keep up regular meditation practice, but I glimpsed it then, and have been returning to it periodically ever since.

Studies on efforts to implement meditation in schools have found that pupils who meditate ten minutes a day can become less anxious, less depressed, less disruptive, and better able to focus. I don't find this at all difficult to believe.

One of the most significant benefits of meditation is that it can enable you to take a back seat to your thoughts for a while. Instead of being at the mercy of whatever nonsense your head decides to conjure up, you can breathe deeply and watch thoughts pass between your ears like fish in an aquarium.

A sixteen-year-old might sit down and find themselves thinking:

Look, there's the anxiety about having not been to the gym this week. Should I go? I guess I could go tomorrow, or. . .

What's Imogen doing? What if she's giving him a blowjob, right now? What if she's rimming him? She never rimmed me. Would I like to be rimmed? Well yes, maybe, is the answer to that, but. . .

*I should eat more vegetables. What was the last vegetable I ate?
I had a tomato on Thursday. A tomato-covered pizza. Does that...*

And breathe.

And breathe.

And by doing this, you start to see your thoughts with some perspective. They are not you, any more than fingernails are you, or your name is you, or your opinion about Marmite is you. By observing them you can strip away their power. A thought is not a truth. A thought is not always something that needs to be heard out. A thought, most of the time, is static generated by a buzzing brain. It's by no means a straightforward thing to grasp, but encouraging your teenager to at least try it might yield some unexpected results.

VII

In the simplest terms, our main task on earth is to keep the people that we love and care about alive. This is why it is so painful when one of these people wants out.

When I was seventeen and recovering from a failed suicide attempt, my mum and I went out to walk the dog. She made me promise not to die.

'Promise me you won't try to die again,' she said.

'I won't,' I told her.

'Good,' she said. 'It's silly and it's selfish. You can't leave me here alone.'

I can understand the impulse to label suicide as selfish. Every time I've tried to commit suicide I've had the thought: it doesn't matter how upset people are, because my lights are going to be off and they're never going to come back on. It doesn't matter if they cry and rage and drink themselves into stupors, because they're going to disappear too, and everything will end, and nothing matters.

Of course, we mostly know not to condemn suicide as selfish, because this looks at it as a moral act rather than a symptom of illness; but it is not always a symptom of illness, and it is far easier to be level-headed about it when it is not your own loved one who has just swallowed sixty-eight paracetamol or leapt off a motorway bridge.

And really, it doesn't matter what suicide is or isn't, just that we try to prevent it with whatever means appear to work. Most well-functioning prevention programmes focus on human connection, safe environments, coping mechanisms, and the introduction of meaning through setting goals. However, as one recent systematic review of prevention programmes in the *Lancet Psychiatry* pointed out, most interventions used on teenagers were originally designed for adults, even though there are so many opportunities to utilize tools such as the internet as a way of getting through to the young. This is where ideas like the panic button app come into their own.

For me, none of the help offered ever really worked. Medication didn't, inept psychologists didn't, and I was certainly not going to call any of the helplines listed in the leaflets we were presented with whenever someone at school paddled across the river Styx.

I wish I had been taught to meditate as a young person, or

at least had a counsellor who could help me to take a step back from the whirlwind of my thoughts and try, with some level of objectivity, to work out which of them was worth listening to. We could all benefit from having nets to catch unhelpful thoughts before they bloom into dangerous behaviours. I'm not touting this as a cure for mental illness, but as a way of trying to make the crushing emotion of adolescence slightly more manageable. We cannot be at the mercy of our thoughts. Our thoughts, especially when we're teenagers, are often very stupid, and in an age where kids are being constantly barraged by new information, finding a way to truly wind down is invaluable.

Saying all that, the last time I tried to kill myself, which admittedly wasn't as long ago as I'd like it to be, I was saved not by any kind of mental karate, but by a shitty shower rail. The first time I tried I was saved by picking up the wrong medication. When it comes to suicide, the banal practicalities can mean the difference between life and death.

After a suicide barrier was erected on the Ellington Bridge in Washington, those wishing to jump off the famous suicide spot didn't just walk to the next bridge, a few hundred metres away; they didn't commit suicide at all. Rates dropped by 50 per cent in the area. And when the gas in British ovens was changed from the perfect poison to a less potent one, it is estimated that six to seven thousand lives were saved over a ten-year period. Suicides in Samoa and Sri Lanka fell dramatically after certain lethal pesticides were banned. Most people who go to commit suicide are not determined to do so at any cost. If you can get even the smallest obstacle in their way, it might well be enough for the impulse to pass, after which they may be more likely to seek some help.

Suicide does not, I think, have to be in the human vocabulary at all. The Pirahā are proof of this. That some teenagers will kill themselves is not something we have to accept, it is something that we have to fight, and statistics make it clear that none of the weapons we're currently using are doing the job. We have to instil in young people the ability to think critically about the media they're presented with and the thoughts that may arise in their brains as a result of it. Suicide is not the beginning of a revenge fantasy. It is not the way you make people care about you. It is not romantic. It is the end of everything. And in this brief window of existence between nothing at all, it means throwing away the only chance you will ever get to meet the universe.

Don't forget:

- This might go without saying, or it might not, but if your teenager ever mentions suicide, treat it with the utmost seriousness. Most people mention suicide at some point before they try it, even if they do so in the guise of a joke. I've said 'I'll just kill myself' as a joke response while thinking of it seriously, just because it's a relief to be able to get it out, however you do it.
- Meditation apps like Sam Harris' Waking up or Headspace can help. They cost a bit of money, but Sam Harris will give anyone free access to his if they send him an email explaining that they can't afford it. All those tricks

developed by social media companies to keep us coming back can also be channelled into helping us develop healthy habits. As well as meditation, there are apps like Stay Alive and Calm Harm that can help in other ways.

- Discourage excessive isolation, encourage exercise, and keep an eye out for changes. Try to talk out anxieties or worries, and don't let arguments extend for any longer than they have to. The sooner you're friends again, the better. Sometimes a young person is having a terrible time outside the home, and an argument within it can be the tipping point.

Homework:

On YouTube, you'll find the full 2006 documentary *The Bridge*, in which Eric Steel filmed the Golden Gate Bridge in San Francisco for a year, capturing a number of suicides. He goes on to interview the friends and family of people who jumped that year. One of the most poignant stories is of a young man who realized, while falling, that he didn't want to die, and tried to rotate himself so he hit the water feet first. In the documentary, he speaks from a wheelchair. He'll never be able to walk again. It's his story that has always sat in the back of my head in desperate moments. What if this goes wrong, but not so wrong that I escape unscathed? What if this only leads me into a life more difficult than the one I had before?

Lesson Eleven:

Asking for Happiness

Locus of control, half-finished brains, and thanksgiving

I

The most helpful thing my mum ever did was get me to talk until I'd thought out my own beliefs. This didn't always happen, it didn't even happen a lot, but the times it did happen stuck with me.

We were once delayed at a train station because someone had thrown themselves onto the tracks a little further down.

'That's so selfish,' I declared. 'If I was going to kill myself, I'd never do it like that.'

'Why do you say that?' my mum asked.

'Because the driver has to watch them splat in his face and some people will see it and they'll all be mentally scarred and late for work.'

'What do you think the person was thinking?'

'I don't know. That they wanted to die.'

'Do you think you can imagine what was going on in their head?'

'I don't know,' I said.

I couldn't. I had only ever tried to kill myself in ways that had a fairly low success rate. Whether this was subconscious or not, I could not comprehend throwing myself to a certain and violent death.

'Do you think the person who jumped in front of the train was thinking clearly?'

'No,' I conceded.

And I kept thinking about it.

I still come back to this conversation today. It's had repercussions. When someone is grumpy, I don't always leap to the conclusion that they're an asshole. I imagine that their partner has recently left them or they've lost a pet or been diagnosed with something painful, life-threatening, or both. There is a reason they're acting that way, I try to think, and it probably doesn't involve trying to make my life more difficult.

This sits in stark contrast to what I remember as one of the less effective parenting techniques she used: after finding a packet of cigarettes, I was sat down and told to smoke them all. I think this was something she'd seen on a TV show. The problem was, it wasn't a full packet. It was maybe four or five cigarettes. I could see the intention was that I'd smoke them and then have to vomit, but it wasn't quite enough. I smoked them and then we sat staring at each other.

'Well,' she said. 'Just don't smoke. You can't smoke.'

(She said this while lighting her own cigarette. It's not hard to see how it took so much legislation to begin curbing the number of smokers in the UK.)

It was a parenting technique that was so obviously a parenting technique, so blatantly someone else's idea of how smoking should be dealt with that it almost hurt to think she thought it would work on me. It sat alongside the naughty step and 'there are children in Africa who would kill for that soggy tuna pasta' as meaningless, unthought-out responses. It was a closing down of communication channels. It was saying, I am right and you are wrong, and I do not have to explain why or enter into a discussion because I am the adult.

There are any number of jokes about children who continually ask their parents, why? Of course it happens, but as important as the answers parents give are the questions they pose. In the same way that Socrates spoke to the people of Athens, the best way to teach people is to get them to think for themselves. You do not change someone's mind by telling them the right answer – the internet is proof enough of this – you change their mind by encouraging them to dig deeper, question more, and learn to think for themselves. Why am I cutting myself? Why can't I look away from my phone? What is making me unhappy? Why do I think a pill might help? In an age when young people are being constantly bombarded with useless drivel, hateful opinions, baseless judgements, and shallow emotional fluff, I can't help thinking that the best thing a parent can do is get teens to think a little more carefully about how they want to respond to things.

II

A 2019 'State of the Nation' report conducted by the Department of Education found that 84.9 per cent of children aged ten to fifteen and 82.9 per cent aged sixteen to twenty-four reported being either happy or very happy with their lives. You must be doing something right! The graphs of the eighty-seven-page report show one particularly interesting finding related to factors tied to the psychological health of teenage girls. (For the purposes of the study, they chose to focus on girls because the study suggests that they are the most at-risk group, with an estimated 25 per cent of girls between eleven and fifteen suffering from an emotional disorder.) The factors that most put them at risk of psychological issues were:

- Online bullying
- Risky behaviours
- Offline bullying
- Spending a lot of time on homework
- Social media use

While those that were most likely to protect them from mental health problems were:

- Physical exercise
- High locus of control
- Positive attitude to school

- Sleeping eight to ten hours
- Seeing friends
- Feeling safe in neighbourhood

These behaviours hark right back to the beginning of this book, when we first looked at how the internet had barged its way into teenage bedrooms and refused to leave. None of the protective factors for psychological health involve phones or computers; in fact a number of them – exercise, seeing friends, sleeping – are activities that often get pushed to one side in favour of time online, especially if you're one of the third of British thirteen-to-fifteen-year-old girls who spend five hours or more a day on social media. Some of the biggest risk factors, however, like cyberbullying and social media use, could be eliminated entirely by making the switch from a smartphone to a dumbphone. Your child might be bullied a little more in school for having a phone that looks like it's come from a nineties sitcom, but apparently this real-life bullying has less of an effect than its online counterpart.

It's no shock that exercise, sleep, friends, and believing you have the power to change things about your life will lead to kids being happier. While the first three problems of the quartet are fairly straightforward, instilling an internal locus of control is the trickiest one.

Locus of control is a concept outlined by Julian Rotter in the fifties to describe the degree of control a person believes they exert over their own life. Before a test, kids with an internal locus of control may say 'If I study hard, I'll do well' or 'If I practise doing old papers, I might be in with a better chance of success.'

Kids with an external locus of control, on the other hand, may think 'I'm shit at maths so I'll fail this test anyway' or 'The test is going to be impossible.' Then, when the test results come in, the internal locusts think 'Well, I did study hard' or 'Fuck, I didn't study enough' while the externals resign themselves 'I fluked that' or 'Mr Rogers marked me way harshly because he still hates me for asking about anal sex last year when they forced him to teach us how babies are made.'

Children with an internal locus of control tend to live happier, more successful lives. A 2008 study, led by Dr Catharine Gale, followed more than 7,500 British people and found that those who had a more internal locus of control at age ten were, by the age of thirty, less likely to be in poor health, showing high levels of psychological distress, or be in a low-paying job.

How do you convince a teenager who may feel that most things are out of their hands, that they are in fact the captain of their own, messy, sock-strewn ship? How do you make them believe that their lives are not shaped primarily by outside forces? Locus of control seems to be at least partly determined by a kid's relationship to their parents. When the parents encourage a child's independence and teach them the relationship between cause and effect, they are more likely to develop an internal locus of control. It is not something that can be instilled overnight but it is something that can be consciously worked towards.

I was not so lucky.

I fell squarely in the camp of external locus of control. As a teenager I was obsessed with the idea that there could be no such thing as free will, that we were simply carried about by our brains, watching them respond to stimuli while being presented with the illusion that we are in the driving seat. Perhaps unhelpfully, I grew up to find a number of neuroscientists who support this view and have scientific research to back it up. But the belief, or the truth, or whatever it might be, is a harmful one, especially to a teenager. You surrender to the world when you think like that. I'm mentally ill, I'm an addict, I'm shy, I'm stupid, I'm whatever, and I can't change it, because it's who I am.

Fortunately, a teenager's brain can be rewired. There are now books for young people, like the wonderful *You Are Awesome* by Matthew Syed, which preach the gospel of growth mindset. This was an idea concocted by the psychologist Carol Dweck after researching attitudes of students towards failure. Those who were willing to learn from their mistakes rather than becoming disheartened by them invariably did better and were happier. In her book *Mindset*, Carol writes that, 'believing that your qualities are carved in stone – the fixed mindset – creates an urgency to prove yourself over and over', while 'in a growth mindset, people believe that their most basic abilities can be developed through dedication and hard work – brains and talent are just the starting point. This view creates a love of learning and a resilience that is essential for great accomplishment.' Similar ideas were also espoused by the psychologist I least enjoyed learning about during A levels,* Albert Bandura, who couched his theory under the heading of

---

* It meant we had to see grainy videos of kids watching while adults whacked a doll called Bobo. The experiment was meant to see whether this would cause the kids to act more aggressively themselves. It did. So never, ever whack dolls called Bobo while your children are watching.

self-efficacy'. Bandura claimed that to succeed, a person needs to believe that they have the ability to alter their own fate. He suggests four ways in which we learn to develop self-efficacy:

- Mastery experiences: or learning to do things and discovering that the harder we work, the better we become at any given task.
- Vicarious experiences: or watching other people either do well or fuck up and then learning from their successes and failures.
- Social persuasion: or being told we're capable of certain things.
- Enhancing physical status, reducing stress, and negative emotions: or staying healthy and fit so that we are capable of pursuing our goals.

In ways like this, you can teach children who might otherwise not believe that they are in control of their lives. Even if this isn't always the case, thinking it is so may help protect them against unhappiness.

I'm very grateful that my mum kept me from going into the doctor alone for as long as she did. I think she had an inkling of what I wanted to say and what I expected to get in return. She wasn't stupid. In retrospect, I can see how much worse things might have been if I'd taken antidepressants from a younger age, if I'd clung even more fiercely to diagnoses of mental ill health, and surrendered any agency I had to change my circumstances. I know I wouldn't have stayed up all night writing the books that

would eventually mean I never had to wrestle with office poli
or learn how to iron a shirt.

III

I don't know if, as a teenager, I had any particular interest in happiness. I had an interest in girls, certain boys, most books, and getting drunk. But I don't think I ever paused to take stock of whether or not I was happy.

Failing to check in with yourself is how we find ourselves in strange places, totally unsure of how we got there. When you're a teenager, you are impatient for your happy chemicals to be unleashed. It is why you jump between intense relationships, engage in risky activities, take drugs and drink. It can lead you into addiction. It can lead you to continuing knocking back psychiatric pills that aren't working. It can lead to you being trapped in abusive relationships. It can lead to you spending six hours a day mindlessly scrolling through other people's posts on your phone. It can be why, in our teenage years, it sometimes becomes almost impossible to feel satisfied with what we have.

I was recently advised by a therapist to start keeping a diary of things for which I was thankful. This was, initially at least, an idea I regarded with outright disgust. Gratitude journals were for smiley Instagrammers, mommy-bloggers, and Christians. Giving thanks was something Americans did during that weird pre-Christmas when they celebrate the slaughter of native people.

But I've come to see the logic behind it.

. don't write much in the diary and I don't write about any-
ing grand or particularly deep, but it is slowly altering the way
I see things. Some days I note down about the tree outside the
window, the *plov* we made for lunch, or the first cigarette I had
in the morning while reading a book of Emily Berry poems. The
longer I do this, the more I begin to notice the things I have to
be grateful for. We can, after all, only see the things we look for.

It's backed up by research too. A study carried out by the psychologists Robert Emmons and Michael McCullough involved
assigning two groups to spend ten weeks either listing things
they were happy about or listing things that annoyed them. The
results showed that those who noted down the things they gave
thanks for were not only more optimistic, but more likely to go
to the gym and less likely to go to the doctor. Being forced to
be grateful had made them healthier and happier. (And that's the
last tangential study I'll bore you with, I promise.)

Ungrateful is a criticism often levelled at the young. Unaware
is probably a fairer adjective. I'm not saying that you're going to
convince Oscar to start his own daily gratitude journal, but I think
there are ways we can try and shift his focus from the things he
doesn't have, the things that have gone wrong, and the things that
might go wrong, to the things that he does have, the things that
have gone right, and the moments when he's enjoyed himself.

Whenever I got home from school, the most common
responses I gave to 'How was your day?' were 'Fine' and 'Shit,
because Mr Carter was a dickhead and Dylan said I took it too
far when we were prodding the dead squirrel with sticks and then
I threw it in Lucy Morgan's face.' If my mum had asked, 'Which

good things happened to you today?' I would have had to work a little harder to muster a response. I didn't really notice good things. Good things tended not to stick. Which isn't to say there weren't any, just that they were lost in the maelstrom of anxieties around exams and bacne and which of my friends were still my friends after squirrelgate. The internet doesn't help matters either. Scrolling through Instagram, you lose any awareness of the things you do have, since all you can see are the things you don't – the enviable body, the gang of glowing friends, the elephant-flattened trainers, the new Supreme hot water bottle.

Armed with the growth mindset of our old friend Carol, though, I'm perfectly willing to believe that, with a little practice, young people can learn to count their blessings and become happier people because of it.

The modern world is filled with tricks designed to keep kids coming back to things that aren't going to make them happy: Snapstreaks, loot boxes, increasingly extreme YouTube recommendations; it's by recognizing this, while taking note of the things that do bring joy, that they may be able to regain control of their lives and slouch a little closer to happiness.

You are the person who is in control of the person they'll become. You are the one who can help them wrestle back their own thoughts, bodies, time, and money from the companies, individuals, and organizations who do not have their best interests at heart. You are the one person who is completely on their side. You are their best shot at being able to take on a world which is changing so rapidly that there is no one who is not struggling to keep up.

IV

I am almost certain my mother would not have even started reading this book. You, on the other hand, have almost finished it. The very fact that you've drudged through more than two hundred pages written by someone as inept and unqualified as me means something. It shows a willingness to learn about the world of the modern teenager, rather than dismiss it as an age of selfishness, self-pity, and laziness. It shows an openness to understanding what is going on with your kids, rather than the inclination to write off their experiences as bizarre, stupid, or unknowable.

In the words of that old guy from that old band, the kids are all right. They have been, they will be, and they are. But no matter how many interracial gangbangs they watch, how much they learn about what is and isn't depression, or how many vital causes they choose to spend their time championing, they are still in possession of unfinished brains, brains that will always believe they know far more than they actually do. In the grand tradition of human beings, these unfinished brains will continue to need guidance from finished brains, like yours. Just because kids have access to all the knowledge of the world through the internet, it doesn't mean that they don't need an adult by their side to help them navigate it.

And adults are all too often doing a hopeless job of it. I don't blame them. The internet is vast and confusing and a lot of the issues of today are far from being resolved. Even the leading finished brains of our time have yet to tell us what we ought to do. Though as a culture we decided a while ago that smacking is bad for children, we've yet to reach such a consensus on porn or social media or how to tell someone not to self-harm without making them want to self-harm even more. The only way we're going to find out the best ways of tackling these things is by listening, by observing, and, most probably, by making a few mistakes.

The teenagers of today have more opportunities than any other group in history to realize their potential. Equipped with knowledge, resources, and the ability to communicate with the entire world, there is no limit to what they can achieve. They're just going to need some help getting over the strange new obstacles that have appeared in their paths. If we can get them safely over these hurdles, I think the planet might be in safe hands.

Don't forget:

- Ask questions. Big questions. The biggest questions. Again and again.
- Help your kids find the things they love, and remind them, as often as possible, how important those things are to them.
- Teach the people you've made that they are in control of their lives. In a world that's feeling increasingly chaotic, knowing they have some measure of power to change things will imbue them with the courage necessary to flourish.

- Always know more than your kids do, especially about the things they think they've got covered.

Homework:

Read a book that starts with a murder and ends with a murder being solved. You've earned it.

Acknowledgements

Thanks to Jan, for coming up with this book, but for everything else, too. Thanks to Katy, for refusing to let the idea go, and for pulling me from the scrapheap. Thanks to Bethany, who may not read this far. Thanks to Mum, of course; I still wish you weren't dead. Thanks to Nan. Thanks to Clive and the Brooks'. Thanks to Big Crispy and Fagin's. Thanks to J and the Williamses. Thanks to Jacek and Skierka. Thanks to D and the Robinsons. Thanks to Dan, Matt, Oscar and everyone else who was fifteen at the same time I was. Thanks to Crispin. Thanks to all the kids who endured painful questions from me during the making of this book. Thanks to Tanya Goodin. Thanks to all at Quercus and Hachette. Thanks to Quinton Winter. Thanks, very much, to Renata. And thanks to everyone I missed out too – it's been a strange few years.